Finding My Way
HOME

Finding My Way Home
A Journey to Discover Hope and a Life of Purpose

All Scriptures unless otherwise noted are NIV. In addition,
there are passages from The Message, NLT, and from KJV.

Published by Forefront Books.

Written in collaboration with Dick Parker.

Cover Design by Bruce Gore, Gore Studio Inc.
Interior Design by Bill Kersey, KerseyGraphics

Cover photo by Meshali Mitchell

ISBN: 978-1-948677-84-4
ISBN: 978-1-948677-85-1 (eBook)

Finding My Way
HOME

A JOURNEY TO DISCOVER HOPE AND A LIFE OF PURPOSE

JOHN HOUSTON

Forefront
BOOKS

TABLE *of* CONTENTS

DEDICATION

I would like to dedicate this book first to Jesus—without Him and His love and faithfulness, I would not have a God story.

And I dedicate this book to my wife, Tracy, and our children, Austin and Ashtyn, for giving me a home full of more love than I ever imagined possible.

FOREWORD

*T*here's a one-letter difference between the words *hope* and *home*, but in the world of my friend John Houston, there's no difference at all.

Home and hope go hand in hand.

I first met John several years ago during a trip to Guatemala. My nonprofit organizations, the John Maxwell Leadership Foundation and EQUIP, were hosting several key business and community leaders to show them the work we are doing to develop transformational leaders and communities across the globe. John's heart for investing in people was immediately apparent, and, as we talked, I learned more about his story.

While he's better known for his successful businesses, John's story doesn't begin with his career; it begins with the tragedy and hardship that shaped his early life. From his parents' divorce to the moment he and his brother found themselves alone and on their own, I listened intently as John shared the ways God took care of him and prepared him for his future.

Eventually, John met his wife, Tracy, and discovered the family he'd never known. Her parents graciously opened their arms to him and taught him that, in the midst of great pain, God offers greater comfort. As John learned to build a loving home with Tracy, he also learned how to become a leader. Over time, as mentor after mentor invested into his life, John turned his growth into an instrument for God's glory.

It's no coincidence that John's career revolves around helping families build their dream home—it's what John has worked toward his entire life. *Finding My Way Home* is John's story, told openly and honestly with the hope of helping others find their way to God. John uses illustrations from his own life that can help you discover and fulfill your God-given purpose and turn your work into a platform for God.

Maybe you've lost hope, or maybe you're wondering if there is a home for you—a place where you truly belong. If that's you, then John Houston has a story you need to read.

Because his story might become your story too.

John C. Maxwell
New York Times Bestselling
Author and Leadership Expert

INTRODUCTION

*E*very day I drive through neighborhoods in Dallas-Fort Worth area and see dozens of signs reminding me of what I do:

John Houston Custom Homes

The first company we started and continue to lead is a homebuilding business. We have several companies now, but people still introduce me as, "John, from John Houston Custom Homes."

"Oh, so you build houses."

"Yes, I do." In fact, our company builds more than six hundred homes every year, and we are continuing to grow.

But is that really who I am? A few years ago, I realized that something about these introductions just didn't sit right with me, so I spent some time in prayer and sensed God saying to me, "John, people often tell you that who you *are* is what you *do*. But that's wrong. That's not who you are, and you need to correct your thinking. You might stop building houses one day. And if you *are* only what you *do*, how could you give that up without believing you've lost your whole identity?" It was a sobering thought, and one that definitely got my attention.

In my heart, I knew God was right. Long before I was the CEO of my companies, I was a child of God. I am also a husband, father, son, and friend.

But what does that really mean? Husband. Father. Son. Friend. Child of God. I thought I knew. I dedicated my life to Christ decades ago. I graduated from Bible college, worked with the youth group and served as a leader in our church, and gave beyond my family's tithe. Yet God was telling me I didn't understand what it meant to be loved as His child and to let that realization influence every single relationship in my life.

He reminded me of times and places where I had been an unforgiving son to my mother, who had taken her own life, and to my father.

After twenty years of marriage, I was certain I knew what it meant to be a husband and a father. Then I sensed God saying to me, "Son, I love you, but you need to understand that you are a condemning, manipulating father and husband. You are leading by law, not by love, because you don't know *how* to love."

The truths and the evidence God revealed to me were crushing.

But then He said gently, "I'm going to teach you. I'm going to show you how to love by revealing My love to you."

This is the story of how God is teaching me—how He has been teaching me all my life by bringing loving, generous, and forgiving people to me and by revealing Himself through His Word.

My father and mother, sister, brother, and I share a painful history that affects each of us differently, and like all family stories, we have different memories. These are my memories and perspective.

It has been a long journey for me as I continue to discover my true identity and let that truth impact every relationship in my life. I see more clearly our parents' love for my siblings and me, and my love for my family grows deeper day by day. As I reflect on the stories here, I realize the irony of God leading me into the homebuilding business. My team and I want to build strong, safe, and beautiful structures for families to create their most cherished memories. But based on my early experiences, I am the least qualified person to truly understand what makes a house a real home with a loving family.

God created a story with my life that puts a spotlight on His mercy and grace—a story of my anger and His forgiveness, of the broken family I grew up in and His restoration, of my demanding "leadership" as a husband and father, and His model for me to lead with love. And because of all He has done for me, I want to help lead others to their eternal home in Him.

I tell that story here, with the hope that you might experience God's infinite love for you and, like me, find your way home.

1

BREAKING APART AND PICKING UP THE PIECES

I was eleven years old the Sunday afternoon that our family fell apart. My sister was twelve, and my brother was fifteen. We were a typical family in a neighborhood of brick ranch houses in Waco, Texas. My brother and I played with kids on our street— sometimes we played tackle football with boys *in* the street. We went to church on Sunday mornings and evenings and on Wednesday nights. If there was anything unusual about our family, it was that I don't remember ever seeing my parents argue.

That Sunday afternoon we came home from a weeklong family vacation and were just getting settled back in when our parents called my brother, sister, and me into the living room. They needed to talk to us.

We all sat down, and they explained that they had wanted to take us on one last trip together as a family. *One last trip?* I thought, confused. *Are we out of money?*

Then they said, "We're getting a divorce," and my head was like, *WHAT??*

The words didn't make sense. What did they mean, "divorce"?

I looked at my brother then my sister to see if they were as confused as I was—or to find some clue that this was a joke I wasn't getting. But nobody was smiling.

Over the next thirty minutes or so, without explaining why, our parents laid out the logistics of the situation. Mom would live somewhere else, and Dad would stay in the house. The three of us would choose which parent we wanted to live with.

How could I make a choice like that? *Right now: Mom or Dad?* I was eleven! How does a kid decide something like that? *Well, Dad sometimes took me deer hunting,* I thought, and I liked to hunt. So that's the best reason I could come up with for saying, "I'll stay with Dad." My brother stayed with Dad, too, and my sister went to live with our mother. That was that.

Except it got worse. Much worse, very soon. Within a few months, our father had married another woman. His new wife had two children of her own, and my brother, Mike, and I didn't necessarily fit into that picture. They actually tried to make us all a family for a while and even moved my sister, Cora, in with us. One day, I walked into the living room just as my stepmother slapped Cora, so I jumped on my stepmother and held her down until our father came home a short while later.

It was obvious that this living arrangement *was not* going to work, so they all moved out—including my father—and Dad let my brother and me live in the house in Waco. My sister moved back in with our mom. This was when my brother and I literally began living on our own. Mike was fifteen and I was eleven.

We basically lived with little-to-no adult supervision. No aunts or uncles or foster parents or anything like that. My older brother was in charge. Our situation was a potential disaster for all of us. Yet I never felt abandoned or even scared. Dad checked on us. Mom called. I always believed in their love for me. They had taught us to be self-reliant since we were very young. Mike and I both hunted deer and dressed everything we killed from the time when we were not much taller than our rifles. With Mike around, I was confident in our ability to make it work.

Lots of kids believe they can take care of themselves. They hear stories about characters such as Mowgli in *The Jungle Book* or the Lost Boys in *Peter Pan* who make it on their own and think, *Yeah, I could do that.* We lived the story in real life. You never know what you *can* do until you *have* to do it, and we did.

Something else happened in those years that I didn't recognize until much later. We were surrounded by good people—godly people—who cared for us from a distance in ways we could not see or even understand at the time.

We had neighbors looking after us. One of our neighbors, Chris, was a college football player, and you can imagine how I idolized him. I was just a kid and yet he truly cared about me. I would even say he loved me. Here's a college kid who could have been doing anything else, but here he was helping me do stuff. For example, I had a project for school where I had to collect and identify dozens of different bugs, and Chris spent a week helping me catch all these bugs, putting them together on a display, and even identifying them. I knew that was special, but when I was older, Chris's gift of time meant even more to me.

The guy living in another house down the street literally sold drugs out his front door. I always saw this guy as the drug lord for our area of town, and yet, for whatever reason, he loved our family. I remember a time while my parents were still together, Mike, Dad, and I were in our front yard one day, and the guy was standing by his truck talking to one of his buyers. The buyer looked over and said something nasty to Dad, and our neighbor grabbed him by the shirt and told him, "You don't ever mess with that family. You talk to him like that again, and I'll take you out."

I can't explain any of that—why so many people cared for us.

People sometimes pray for a "hedge of protection" around themselves or the people they love. The phrase comes from the Old Testament book of Job and describes how God protected Job early in his life before all his troubles began. Well, God must have put a hedge of protection around us. There's no other explanation.

TWO BOYS ON LAWNMOWERS

I think for our age, Mike and I did pretty well and actually prospered financially. We stayed in school, went to church, started a business, later moved into a townhouse apartment, and avoided giving in to most of the temptations that teenage boys face.

Mike had started a landscaping company with a truck and equipment that Dad gave him. Mike was still only fifteen at the time, but he had gotten a hardship driver's license, which you could do in Texas back then. Almost every morning before school, we got up before daylight and mowed lawns. Mike ran the riding mower and the edger, and I had the push mower and trimmer. When we were done, he dropped me off at my middle school and he went to high school. Then he picked me up after school and we worked until dark. That's how we survived.

It sounds crazy looking back on it, but nobody called the state or the county social services to check on us. We weren't making any trouble—we were too busy mowing lawns—and we stayed in school, so I guess nobody saw any reason to report us.

We grew the lawn service business over time, contracting with the owners of duplex apartments to maintain entire developments, thirty or forty at a time. We hit one and moved on to the next. We bought more equipment and started hiring employees to help us. At one point, we had several crews working on more than two hundred yards every ten days. We charged

$35 per lawn, and Mike was good at collecting the money and managing the books. Some of our clients contracted with us to maintain shrubs and flowerbeds, and we sometimes installed landscaping. Those were good projects, but they slowed us down. Our bread and butter was "mowing and blowing."

My brother handled the relationships with clients while I hit up other houses around the neighborhood and passed out flyers for our business. Waco is a tight-knit community, and a business lives or dies by referrals. It was tough to start a business if you weren't from there, but two hardworking teenagers caught people's attention, and they were ready to put us to work.

Mike had a system for maintaining our equipment. We bought high-quality mowers, and we both knew how to repair anything that broke. We kept replacement parts and engines, so if a machine went down, it didn't stay down long. We got it fixed and back in service quickly, generally by the next day.

We drove to school each day with the equipment in the back of the truck or loaded up on a trailer. It was a different world then. We didn't worry about anybody taking our stuff; we were just thinking of the time we'd save by not having to run home for our equipment before making our after-school rounds.

CHURCH AND CHURCHY PEOPLE

Believe it or not, we kept going to church during that time, but that was the one place where we felt a little weird about our living situation. In many ways, we believed we were outcasts. I remember going to church on a Sunday night after I'd been hunting, and somebody told me, "Son, you need to go home and change clothes before you come to church." It only takes *one* of those comments when you're a kid to turn you off, especially when you're already a little cynical about the church and its "churchy" people. I didn't go home and change clothes that night—and I started using a different entrance door from that time on to avoid the person who made the comment—but I also never forgot it.

Everybody knew my parents were divorced and that our dad had been involved with another woman at church. After the divorce, several married men from church showed up at our mother's door to try to date her, and my sister saw all of that. She was about thirteen then, and it had a really negative impact on her relationship with God and the church. Some people assumed since my brother and I were living alone, our parents were divorced, and my mom had become an alcoholic, that we must be drinking, partying, and sleeping around. But we were just surviving.

Looking back, I know most of those people were good people. They really did love God, and I don't think they meant to send the message I was receiving. They were focused almost completely on leading someone to Christ—"getting them saved"—and then moving on to the next person, often to the exclusion of developing personal relationships.

Every Sunday, though, one man stood at the back door of the church until I arrived, and he invited me to sit with his family. Danny Kent and his wife had been my kindergarten Sunday School teachers, and he had a heart for me. He was a big, burly guy with a bushy beard, always gentle and loving, and he owned a plumbing company. I never accepted his invitation to sit with them in church—I always sat behind them—but he asked me every week. That meant a lot, more than I realized at the time. I needed to see adults modeling the love of Christ, and Danny Kent did that for me.

A ROYAL RANGER RINGER

Even though we spent most of our after-school hours on lawnmowers, we still made time for other things. Mike and I both played varsity soccer, and we were active in the youth group at our Assembly of God church.

Our youth group was kind of a wild bunch sometimes. The people living in the house next to the church disliked us so much that they named their dog—a vicious German shepherd—*Satan* just to spite us.

To be fair, we gave them plenty of reason not to like us. The neighbors had a fence around their yard that backed up to the church. The fence had a dual purpose: keep Satan in and keep church kids out. They also had a peach tree near the house. That peach tree was a temptation, of course, and we had a game where we tried to jump the fence, run to the tree and grab a peach, and get back over the fence before Satan realized what was happening and came after us. I never got caught, but Satan nipped a couple of guys before they escaped. Even now, I laugh when I read the Bible's depiction of Satan as "prowling around" and "looking for someone to devour" (1 Peter 5:8). Satan was certainly prowling around and trying to devour our youth group! After he got the second guy, we decided to find another game. (There may be a sermon in there somewhere.)

Back then, Assemblies of God churches had a program for teenagers called Royal Rangers. We went on campouts where we competed with boys from other churches, and Mike was great at that stuff. So great, in fact, that the Royal Rangers leader from another church a few miles away called Mike one week to recruit him. He asked if we would consider joining *their* Royal Rangers group and compete with them at the next weekend campout.

The guy didn't know that we were experienced businessmen and that Mike was a great negotiator. He just wanted a ringer to guarantee victory for his youth group.

Mike asked him, "What'll you do for us if we come?"

"What do you want?" the guy said.

"Well," Mike said, "how about steak dinners at the campout?"

"We can do that," he said.

The next weekend, we packed our gear and went to the campout with the other church and won everything. Mike was great and so were the steaks. I think the other guys were happy to have us for a successful weekend, but we were ready to get back to our home church the next week.

After experiences like that, I began to have a skeptical view in my young mind about a Christian's approach to life and business. I started to think success was about the win, about doing what you had to do to make it happen.

OUR MOTHER'S DEPRESSION

About this time, our mother moved to Nashville to write country music. She had some success composing songs about the heartache and the pain she was feeling in her soul. She dealt with her depression by writing about it, drinking way too much, and calling me sometimes.

I was twelve years old the first time she called and told me she was going to kill herself. I didn't know what to do with that information. I told my brother, and we both talked to her and tried to calm her down. All of that ended up in her music. It bothered me that people longed to hear the terrible heartache, pain, and tragedy in her life played out in her music.

Mom sold a few songs, and she worked on a few with Charlie Pride and the Gatlin Brothers, but she knew nothing about business or how to manage money. Instead of investing in herself and bettering her life, she bought lottery tickets. So she was always broke, waiting for the big win that never came. I remember this season very well; these were the times she was the most depressed. She would call me—and she had almost always been drinking—crying, brokenhearted, and ready to take her own life. I didn't know how to help her. It was times like this that I felt so lost and helpless with no idea what to do, what to say, or even where to go for real help.

Even though I was at church all the time, I don't remember praying much as a kid, but I do remember particular moments when I felt the presence of God. For example, I went to church camp once when I was thirteen years old. While I was there, I experienced a moment when I felt the power and warmth and peace of the Holy Spirit like I had never felt it before. That encounter with the Lord impacted my life in ways I did not understand at the time, but I've carried it with me ever since.

If that moment had grown into a deeper relationship with God that I could have understood as a kid, maybe I could have shared His comfort, truth, and healing with my mother. She was divorced and lonely, and she didn't know where to turn. I was beginning to understand, but I wasn't capable of explaining the fullness of God's love to her.

CRUISING IN WACO

Ever since I was a little boy, I've loved fast cars and fast trucks. There is nothing like the feel of a really powerful car or truck that responds to my commands. Around the time I got my driver's license in 1986, my dad bought Mike and me a 1970 Chevrolet pickup for $1,000. He knew we *needed* it for the lawn business, and he knew we would *like* it because it was customized for speed. It had a 327 engine with a three-speed transmission, and the previous owner had bored out the cylinders, making them a little larger and adding horsepower.

Around that same time, my brother bought a 1985 Camaro Z-28, which he later gave to me. I would take the T-tops off and cruise Valley Mills Drive in Waco, driving down and back over and over again along with a thousand other teenagers trying to look cool.

The fast truck and sports car were big deals to me back then. They became an important part of my identity. I loved having people come up to me asking about those cars, talking to girls, and having a girlfriend. It all made me feel like I was valued. I felt so grown-up and special when people found out I lived on my own or when they told me what a cool car I had. Those comments gave me pride and confidence.

Then, at the end of every day, I went home alone.

Mike and I lived in the townhouse together until 1987, when he got married and moved into another apartment complex. I was only sixteen, but I was *officially* on my own at that point. Finances were still tight, but a family from church owned the complex. I think they must have been taking it easy on me for the rent.

Despite the new living arrangement, Mike and I continued to work together all day, every day. The lawn business was doing well, but we needed to make more money (or maybe we just *wanted* more money). It was hard to cut yards after dark, so when we got a chance to clean office buildings at night, we jumped on it. We'd work on lawns during the day and clean offices five nights a week.

Picture it: At sixteen years old, I had cash in my pocket, no adult supervision, and plenty of opportunities to make bad decisions. Sometimes those "opportunities" literally knocked on my door. One Friday night around 11:00 p.m., for example, I'd just gotten home from my office-cleaning job when somebody knocked at the door. I opened it to find a cute girl from high school standing in my doorway. She said, "Hey, I know you're here by yourself. I just came over to see if … maybe … you wanted to have sex?"

Looking back, I have no idea what came over me in that moment. But the first words out of my mouth were, "That's about the *dumbest* thing I've ever heard." There's a chance I might have been even *less* polite than that. The girl in the doorway turned beet red, huffed, and stormed off.

As soon as I closed the door, I thought, *Why did I do that? What sixteen-year-old guy, without parents around, does that?*

I say this with all humility: it had to be God's protection. It made no sense at the time, but today I'm so thankful I shut the door on that bad opportunity that night. From a young age, I knew I wanted to save sex for marriage and *only* for marriage. I knew firsthand the pain that sexual irresponsibility had caused me and so many others, and I wanted nothing to do with it.

A lot of kids see their parents make bad choices and then repeat the cycle by making those same bad choices for themselves. I have definitely done that in a few areas...but not with sex. I can say with confidence that God was watching over me here, even though I didn't recognize it fully at the time.

GENEROSITY BEYOND MY UNDERSTANDING

When I was a senior in high school, an older man I knew in the landscaping business told me, "Son, I highly encourage you to get out of that kind of work and get into something else, because you're not going want to do it when you're older. It's going to wear out your body. It's good money for you now, but it's not sustainable, and it's not going to take you where you want to go." I knew he was right and needed to figure out what my next move would be.

By that time, Mike and his wife had moved an hour and a half away to Irving, Texas, to start a new career. I graduated high school and tried junior college, but I just didn't feel like college was for me. That's when Leonard, the father of a girl I had dated, offered me a job with his vending machine business. It seemed like a good opportunity, so I passed my list of lawncare customers over to some other guys, sold off my lawn equipment, and made my first major career change from lawncare to vending machines.

I started off just working around the warehouse, but that led to running one route, then two. I would go in around 4:00 in the morning and work until noon, driving all over town checking and refilling vending machines.

I didn't know what to do with myself getting off work at noon, so I asked for another shift, which kept me busy until early evening. I was working twelve to sixteen hours a day, five and sometimes six days a week servicing vending machines. Leonard and his wife also did some catering, and they let me help set up and serve. And if he had a weekend shift available, I took that too. All this extra work made a huge impact on me financially. This family took me in as one of their own, and I realized I'd never been loved quite like that before.

One day, I came into the office after my morning shift and Leonard and his wife Sherry pointed to two thirty-gallon trash bags. I opened them up, and they were filled with brand-new clothes they had bought for me. Pants, socks, shoes, underwear, coats—everything. They'd done all this shopping for me.

I can't remember if it was Leonard or Sherry, but one of them said, "We just want you to know we love you and want to help you." It meant far more than they ever knew.

Honestly, I didn't understand their generosity. I thought generous people were "supposed" to be Christians, but as far as I knew, Leonard and Sherry weren't. They just loved me, and they showed that love through their actions. That began to open my eyes and my heart to the possibility that the Lord might someday give *me* an opportunity to be an instrument of His generosity.

"CALL TRACY MILLER"

I was nineteen years old, working a lot, and going home alone. I would have a date here and there, but I was really starting to feel the loneliness that came with being on my own for so long. I was tired and wanted a family, and I said to God, "There's got to be more to life than this. I can't keep coming home to nothing every day."

That was the first time I remember talking to God like that.

I said, "God, You've got to give me a wife or something. What am I supposed to do? Who am I supposed to call?"

For the first time in my life, I felt I heard the voice of God in my spirit. He said, "Call Tracy Miller."

"Dude," (yep, that's how I communicate with God), "I can't do that!" I said out loud. "She's fifteen years old! You must have missed on that one."

Tracy was in my church's youth group, and I had known her for years. For a couple months off and on, I "dated" her best friend and she "dated" my best friend. (I put *dated* in quotes because dating was just hanging out together with the youth group.) I liked Tracy a lot, but she was so young. I pushed back against the idea, but I felt in my spirit this was God speaking to me. So I called her up and asked if she would go out with me.

She said, "Yes."

Her father said, "No." Her brother said, "No way!" But Tracy's mother, Sue Miller, felt differently.

A Mother's Prayers

The first time I saw John was at church when he was five or six years old running around chasing a little girl. Tracy was just a baby. We knew John all those years, and I knew John's family and his situation—that he had been living without a family in an apartment across from the high school.

When Tracy was little and we put her to bed at night, we always prayed for her. At the same time, we prayed for her future spouse, for God to protect him and give him wisdom. So when it came time for her to start dating, I trusted God to protect Tracy, and I felt Him give me peace about John.

— *Sue Miller*

We went on our first date on Valentine's Day. I still remember it like it was yesterday. She was so beautiful (and still is). We went to a Mexican restaurant and then came back to her house to watch a movie with her parents. From the first date, I knew there was something different about this girl, and—for the first time in a long time—I knew my life was starting to change for the better.

2

MODEL SERVANTS

*A*s Tracy and I started dating and I spent more time with her parents and brother, I noticed something different about her family, especially her dad. Steve Miller had a servant's heart, and I did not understand it at all. When Tracy's uncle took her brother and cousins hunting, Steve stayed home with the girls. He loved making late-night ice cream sundaes for them, even if it meant running out to the store for ice cream. And the kids' birthdays were a big deal for him. He always brought home the biggest cake he could find.

I didn't experience that as a kid, so it was weird to see a man serving other people—especially girls. (Yes, I know how that sounds, but it was all I had known up to that point.) If I was going to spend my life with Tracy—and that's what I wanted to do—then I had to learn to be more like her father, the man she loved more than any other. So I watched him serve other people and tried to make sense of it.

Around that same time, God brought another member of our church into my life. Wayne Andersen was a volunteer youth leader, and I helped him with the group. Wayne had a true servant's heart; he would do anything for other people. In addition to volunteering with the youth, he cleaned the church facilities at night—just because he loved the church.

Wayne was a custom homebuilder, and he offered me a job doing framing and concrete work. I could make more money doing that, and it seemed like there was more career potential for me there than running vending machines, so I took it. It was harder work, from early morning to late night, but I enjoyed it. Plus, I was learning a lot about construction. After work, I also helped him with custodial chores at church. It was good for me to spend time with Wayne and his family. He gave me more opportunities to learn how to lead and serve while I was learning the skills of a trade.

A NEW HOME, A NEW FAMILY

One night, I came home to my apartment after a long, hard, and hot day of work to find a bunch of police cars in the parking lot. I had a roommate by this point—a guy from church who moved in with me to help pay the bills—and I was about to discover that my roommate was having a very bad day. Officers were standing right outside my apartment with my front door open.

It took a while before anyone would tell me they were arresting my roommate. Apparently, he had created a scheme to steal money by manipulating invoices and merchandise at the jewelry store where he worked.

Over the next few days while I was figuring out what had happened and what I should do, Tracy's parents sat me down in their living room and said, "We prayed about your situation at the apartment, and we believe the Lord is saying you should come live in our home with us."

This was beyond anything I could have imagined. I knew they were generous and trusted me, but to invite their daughter's much-older boyfriend to come live in their home? That crossed into unknown territory. I was witnessing greater love and trust than I could understand.

You can imagine that moving me into their home wasn't going to be a popular decision for the Millers at church, with their extended family, or even for Tracy at school. She was a junior in high school, and we'd been dating for almost a year. I still hadn't told her that I loved her, though I knew three months after we started dating that I would ask her to marry me someday.

I also knew the reputation I had at school and at church because I had been living on my own. My family's and my reputation would spill over onto Tracy behind her back. People were bound to whisper about the Millers letting their daughter's twenty-year-old boyfriend live in their house.

But Steve and Sue believed they were faithfully serving the Lord by taking me in. Looking back, I am confident they were. I reflect on that time living with them as one of the most transformative times of my life, seeing a properly functioning family—husband, father, wife, mother, son, daughter—interact every day.

Tracy also believes the timing of our coming together protected her. "God probably brought John into my life at the right time," she says, "because some of my friends started partying around then. I had gone out with them a little bit, but then I started dating John and suddenly wasn't as interested in partying anymore. Now I look back and realize God was also looking out for me."

I had never seen a family function as theirs did. It was strange to me. Sometimes it even seemed fake. I would often wait for the big fight, the big dysfunction, the unfaithfulness, the broken trust—all the junk I assumed every family kept buried—but it never came. When they disagreed, they actually *talked it out*. It felt too good to be true, so I sometimes convinced myself that it was.

The Lord used that experience to start a deep stirring in my heart. I was receiving exactly what I had asked God for when I prayed, "God, there has to be more to life than this." He was showing me that there truly is more in Christ—that His desire was to bring redemption, reconciliation, and restoration to every area of my life. Their model, as much as any experience in my life, prepared me to be a godly husband and father and to come to know God as a true heavenly Father.

SEEING TRUST IN ACTION

My dates with Tracy consisted mostly of hanging out with the youth group. On Sunday nights, the group almost always went to Poppa Rollo's for pizza. It was a gigantic restaurant with an arcade and TVs that showed old episodes of *The Three Stooges*, *The Little Rascals*, and *Laurel and Hardy* or *Popeye* cartoons. The place was always filled with families. When Tracy's parents let me take her out alone, we kept going back to Poppa Rollo's, and then we went back to her house to watch a movie, often with her parents. That extended time with Steve and Sue was such an important time in my life. Seeing their interactions intrigued me. They were loving and trusting, and I wanted a family like that.

I was there one night when Tracy's mom hung up the phone and said, "Steve's going to be a little late. He got tied up at the office." *Finally*, I thought, *a crack*. Reality was about to break through.

I thought, *Hah! I can't believe she's actually buying that lame excuse!* I had never seen a faithful relationship, so I asked her, "Do you really believe that? Don't you know what he's *really* doing?"

I can still see the look on her face—not angry or condemning, but *sad*. She truly felt sorry for me in that moment because my gut reaction was to assume the worst, even about someone I loved and trusted. It hit me that I didn't understand how to have a marriage built on trust. I had a lot to learn. I was excited about the *idea* of being married to Tracy and being part of her family, but was I really willing to put in the work to change the thought patterns and beliefs that were so rooted in my soul? Could I get to a point where I could be a spiritual leader to Tracy and our family? This thought scared me, but I believed at that moment that I *would* do it. I knew without a doubt that I *wanted* to.

After I moved in with her family and Tracy, I became more serious about our relationship, and I sometimes questioned whether Tracy was the one I should marry. Was this what the Lord wanted? Did she want the same things I did, and would she fight alongside me to get them? I wasn't that spiritually mature at the time, so I didn't even know where to look for answers to these questions. What I *did* know was I was hungry for God and His Word, and so was Tracy. We studied the Bible and prayed together. I loved her heart and drive to follow Christ, as well as her willingness to work to find the answers. I loved that she loved her family and wanted a family of her own one day. I was confident the Lord was calling us together and that we could create a future together.

There was no doubt. She was "the one."

MOVING UP THE TIMETABLE

In the summer before Tracy's senior year in high school, I felt the Lord saying He wanted us to get married and go to Bible college. I mentioned that to Tracy, and she said she felt the same way. We talked with her parents about getting married the following summer after she graduated, and that became the plan.

Then in October, as we were going through the process of applying for college and financial aid, Tracy's dad discovered that the grants we could receive as a married couple would be a lot better than we could get as individuals. This was a big deal because neither Tracy's nor my parents could help pay for our college. Then, in one of those life-changing moments, Tracy's parents sat us down and said, "We think it makes the most sense for you to go ahead and get married sooner than later since it will help with college grants."

They were expressing a level of trust in me that I had never experienced. Sure, they had given us their blessing to get married the following summer after Tracy graduated from high school, but that seemed so far away. Now they were giving me permission to marry their daughter in just two months! I understood even then that their trust in me reflected their trust in

God, who had assured them that He, too, blessed our marriage and would protect us. I vowed to Tracy, to them, and to God not to betray that trust.

We discussed it and decided to get married during the Christmas break of her senior year of high school. It was the best Christmas gift ever! So with only two months until December, we needed to make a plan quickly.

Of course, that's when people at church and in the community *really* started talking. I mean, what kind of couple would you *expect* to get married in high school? Pregnant couples. Even though we'd never had sex, the word on the street was that Tracy was pregnant. Seeing as how we didn't have a child for another five years, I guess the community finally came to believe us at some point.

MODELING TRUST AGAIN

One night, we were addressing wedding envelopes when the phone rang. Tracy's dad got a call from a woman at work, and he went to use the phone in the kitchen. Tracy's mom came back and picked up another envelope. I didn't understand. She must have noticed I was looking at her oddly, because she asked me what I was thinking.

"Aren't you going to listen to what they're saying?" I said.

"Why?" she asked. "Are you still doubting Steve and his faithfulness?"

Before I could answer, she said, "Steve has never given me a reason not to trust him. He's taking care of his business on the phone, and there's no reason for me to listen."

"Well, if that were at my house," I said, "that phone would have been thrown across the room."

Despite my lack of trust and my family's history, Tracy's parents continued to believe in me. They were praying daily that God would work on my heart and build in me the loyalty and honor that a lifelong commitment to their daughter would require. I was a work in progress, and it was God who was doing the work. Today, decades later, I wonder if I would trust the twenty-two-year-old me with my teenage daughter. Would I trust God to transform that young man the way Sue and Steve trusted Him? I thank God that He hasn't tested me on that one.

During that time living in the Millers' house, I saw day after day what a husband and wife should look like, what a dad and a mom should sound like, and what a loving home felt like. God showed me in those days how a family should operate with the love of Christ. I still didn't fully understand, but I did get a new perspective I would later appreciate and utilize.

SETTING THE PILLARS PROPERLY

Tracy's parents gave us $2,000 for the wedding and said we could keep whatever we didn't spend. That was a pretty good chunk of money for us in 1993, and we wanted to save as much as we could. We got married in our church, which didn't allow dancing then, and that was fine with us. So the reception was pretty much cake and punch.

Friends of Tracy's mother arranged the flowers. Tracy rented her dress, which saved a lot. I had a bright idea that saved a little more on the wedding cake—but that one almost backfired on me. We ordered it from a woman about thirty miles away, and she said she'd deliver it and set it up for an extra $25.

"No thanks," I said. "We need that $25."

Tracy disagreed. She had visions of me ruining our wedding cake by trying to set it up myself, and she insisted that we let the lady deliver it.

Later that afternoon I thought, *How hard can it be?* I called the baker back and said, "We won't need you to deliver the cake after all. I'll come pick it up and set it up myself."

So on the morning of our wedding day, I picked up the cake and she showed me how everything fit together before boxing it up. When I got to the church, I took everything out of the box and assembled our wedding cake on the table in the fellowship hall. It was easy and looked great! Best of all, I had saved a little money.

As I was admiring my handiwork, I heard a woman behind me exclaim, "Oh, my goodness!"

I turned around and saw a friend of Tracy's mom looking intently at the cake.

"John," she said, "you've got the pillars upside down."

"Does that matter?" I asked.

"Of course, it matters!" she said. "If somebody tries to cut that cake, the whole thing will come crashing down! I'm just glad I saw it before the wedding."

My guardian angel took the cake apart for me and reassembled it correctly, and the wedding and reception went smoothly.

I came to realize sometime later that I was attempting to build our marriage and our future home with the pillars upside down. I had gone behind Tracy's back and betrayed her trust in me, believing I knew better, just to save a few dollars. How would that work out over the years?

We lived with Tracy's parents for another eight months after the wedding, and God continued to use Steve and Sue to model His love and grace. But as you can see, I was a slow learner.

A FIXER-UPPER

In the fall, after Tracy graduated high school, we both enrolled in Southwestern Assemblies of God University (SAGU) and rented a little duplex right across from campus for $275 a month. The owner didn't want to rent to students, but he let us have it. Looking back, I know it was definitely the Lord helping us.

The house wasn't without its problems, though. It had no insulation, and by Thanksgiving, the gaps in the windows and doorframes were letting cold air blow in. We hung blankets on the back wall of the bedroom to cut the drafts in winter. Two of the three rooms had little unvented Dearborn gas space heaters, but we were afraid to leave them running all night. So I got up early every morning and lit the heaters to warm the house for an hour before Tracy got up.

As cold as we were in the winter, we were even more uncomfortable in the summer. With no insulation *or* air conditioning, the little house baked us alive. We came home one afternoon and saw that the candles Tracy had used to decorate had melted and drooped in the heat. That's not exactly what you want your bride to experience. Texas heat can be rough, and we had to figure something out fast.

I told the owner I would install insulation throughout the house if he would buy it. He went along with the idea, so I rented the blower machine and got the insulation. Our plan was for me to blow in the insulation throughout the attic while Tracy kept the machine fed outside. I filled it up for her the first time before going upstairs. It was smoking hot that day, and I wanted to finish as fast as possible, so I got after it. Before long, the insulation stopped blowing.

I thought, *What the heck is she doing?* How could Tracy leave me cooking in the attic like that? I climbed down the ladder to push her along, and she had gone inside. I went in the house and saw she was lying on the couch struggling with an asthma attack triggered by the insulation floating out of the bags.

"What are you doing?" I asked. "Get back out here so we can finish the job!" Let's just say, it was not my shining moment. She was really struggling, and I didn't show much empathy. When it finally dawned on me that Tracy wouldn't be able to help, I decided to make another plan.

I called my dad and he came over and helped the following weekend. I finished our half of the duplex with no trouble before slowly crossing over to our neighbor's side in the attic to keep blowing insulation. A short while later, my foot slipped off a joist and I fell through the ceiling into their living room! I was able to catch myself, but our neighbors and their friends jumped out of the way as I hung by the joist in their living room. "Good morning!" I said, not sure what else to say.

I hollered at Dad to come in, and he surveyed the damage. He was better at repairing sheetrock than I was, so he got it fixed pretty quickly.

This was a tough season being newly married, broke, and living in a small, old duplex. I was starting to see how some of my thought processes and upbringing didn't affect just *me* anymore. It was impacting Tracy as well.

3

LEARNING TO
HEAR GOD'S VOICE

*I*n my first semester of Bible class, the professor explained a misconception in the church today. He said we think we're called to *get people saved*—to encourage people to accept Christ as their Savior—but that's not true. He explained that God actually calls us to *make disciples*, and that's a different thing altogether.

My first thought was, *That's blasphemy! It's not even biblical.* But then we read the Scripture, and I realized he was right. Jesus said, "Go and *make disciples* of all nations" (Matthew 28:19). That realization rocked my world because I had been taught one thing my whole life, but here was a whole different concept. This challenged me and made me wonder what else had I been taught that wasn't biblical. This may not seem like a big deal to some, but it was huge for me. Remember, I had grown up already having issues with the church and Christians. This was a trust issue. If I had been taught something that wasn't really what Jesus said, what else had I been taught that was wrong?

I knew from that point on I had to learn the Word of God way better than I ever had. I had a deep hunger to find biblical truth. I wanted to be a disciple.

A professor had told us we could pray and ask God to speak to us, and He would. I looked it up in John

10:3–4, and there it was: "The gatekeeper opens the gate for him, and the sheep listen to his voice. He calls his own sheep by name and leads them out. When he has brought out all his own, he goes on ahead of them, and his sheep follow him because they know his voice."

I was learning so much, so fast. We had chapel every day, and then I would go back to our duplex to pray and listen for God to speak to me. And every day, I ended my prayer time with disappointment, saying, "God, you didn't speak to me today." I was growing incredibly frustrated spiritually and thinking I just wasn't holy or good enough. Maybe this is a *me* issue because of things I'd done or my family had done. Maybe I would never have that kind of relationship with the Lord.

Then within a day or two of hitting my lowest point, I went to chapel and that day's speaker stepped up and said, "You know what? I think I'm going to go a different route than what I planned today. I really feel like the Lord is telling me that there are people in here who want to hear the voice of God, but they don't know how. And I feel like God wants me to keep it simple and teach you how to hear what He has to say."

I sat up straight and listened, thinking maybe this guy had the answer for me. Over the next few minutes, he broke it down in a way I could finally understand.

"We way overcomplicate hearing the voice of God," he said.

He told us to get a journal or something else to write on—he suggested a notebook so we could keep track of it by date. "Go into a room and begin to pray, simply talking to the Lord like you would a spouse or close friend. When you finish praying," he said, "sit quietly. Then start writing down everything that comes to your mind—everything you're thinking."

"After you do that," he continued, "see if what you've written lines up with the Word of God. If it lines up with the Word, there's a fifty-fifty chance it's God speaking to you. But guess what? God is not going to condemn you if you make a mistake while you're trying to hear His voice and follow Him. If you are genuinely and consistently trying to hear His voice, will that please Him? Of course, it will!"

When I first started doing this, I would write a line and immediately ask, "Is this God or is this me?" I quickly learned that wasn't a good way to do it. My prayers were too chopped up. Instead, I just prayed.

When my prayer ended, I sat quietly and started writing when something popped into my head. I kept writing until I felt like I had captured everything I sensed God saying to me.

Then I worked through everything I had written, line by line, and compared it to Scripture. If it didn't line up with the Bible, I struck through it, because that was me. If I found that what I had written lined up with the Bible, I left it.

At first, since I didn't know the Bible well enough, I often felt stuck and had questions after studying, so I asked other people to help me. I was willing to do anything to keep learning. It turned out that about 20 percent of what I had written lined up with Scripture, and about 80 percent didn't.

I set a goal of praying and writing like that five times a week. Over the months, as I spent more time reading Scripture and praying, my writing lined up more often with what God had said.

I was doing it. I was learning to hear my Father's voice.

When our son was born a few years later, God gave me a perfect picture of what this must have looked like from His perspective. Tracy had literally just given birth, and the doctor was holding our son, Austin. I said something to Tracy, and Austin turned his head toward me. Even though he had never seen me, he had been hearing my voice for months, and he recognized it. Fast-forward a few years, and Austin was in kindergarten. I went to his Sunday School room and stood at the door watching twenty children running around. I said, "Austin," and only one child looked up. My son. He recognized my voice even with everything else going on in the room.

Now, suppose you have a son or daughter who plays football or is a cheerleader. You're in the stands, and they're out on the field. There may be hundreds of people in the stands yelling, but they recognize your voice even in the midst of that crowd. Then they're in college, maybe in another state, and they're facing a difficulty, maybe even temptation. And in an instant, they have a thought, *What would Dad or Mom say right now?* They think about what you have told them in the past and hear your voice.

That's how the Spirit of the Lord works. With so many things going on, you can still hear and recognize His voice. If you first learn to hear Him during your one-on-one time with God in that quiet room with the door closed, then you'll still hear and recognize His voice no matter where you are or what is going on.

Understanding that I could hear the voice of God and having a method for doing that changed the trajectory of my life. My prayer time became more personal and more intimate. I began to dig deeper into the Word of God, because that's the only way I had to confirm if what I was hearing was from Him. It seems crazy to me that I grew up in church and no one ever taught me how to do this. But over the years, I have come to realize that the Word of God gives me a foundation of truth for every decision I need to make. The more I study and know His Word, the more the Holy Spirit has the opportunity to speak to me through what I am reading. God's heart and character are all laid out in the Scriptures for me to follow.

Now, nearly twenty-five years later, I'm still trying to hear His voice more intimately and clearly. My goal is to start the day with prayer and Scripture at least five days a week. If I don't do that first, I feel lost, quickly get distracted, and start my day off running in the wrong direction.

When I was a kid growing up in Waco, we had a neighbor who gave a model for this type of discipline.

He was a marathon runner, and his daughter and I were friends. One day when she and I were playing outside, he came out to stretch before a run.

He walked over to us and said, "I want to talk to you guys for a second and maybe teach you something I hope you'll remember when you grow up."

I listened, because I was so impressed that he was a competitive runner. He said, "When I'm training for a race, I have to push myself hard. Some days, I run twelve or fifteen miles or even longer. That's what it takes to prepare to run a marathon. Then there are some days when I just run two or three miles for whatever reason. And that's okay. I can take a day off here and there. But when I do, I know I can't give myself the same option tomorrow. Tomorrow, I have to push myself back up to fifteen miles again."

I've carried that lesson now for more than forty years, and I use it in several areas of my life, including my prayer life. I don't make myself spend an hour in my prayer room seven days a week, but I know if I go more than a couple of days in a row without having dedicated prayer time, reading His Word and listening to His voice, then my attitude and thought processes start to change. I went down some bumpy roads to learn that the more observant I am of my morning time with God, the better I am at making wise decisions, having healthy relationships, and being successful in every area of my life.

I'm not saying this is for everybody; I'm just saying this is what God has taught me about me. I have to put some non-negotiables on my schedule, whether I'm at home or traveling. Even if we're on vacation with the kids, they come in and pray with us.

Most mornings I'm up around 5:00 a.m. to work out. I listen to Scripture while doing cardio and ask God, "What do you want to speak to me through your Word?" I'm an auditory learner so listening helps.

As I am writing this book, God has me going through the book of John. I've read it several times over about six months, and then He directed me to chapters 13, 14, 15, and 16 over and over again. Sometimes one or two verses will stick out.

When I get home from the gym, I shower and dress, and then I go to my prayer room. It's a particular place in our house that we've dedicated to prayer, and that's where I study whatever verse God has given me for the day. I pray and ask the Lord to speak to me regarding what He is trying to tell me, teach me, or reveal to me through that passage of Scripture.

There was a time when I became legalistic about my prayer time, and before long it became a box for me to check off every day. God corrected me on that. Now it's a time I look forward to and enjoy in the morning. There are definitely times when it's a struggle, but on those days I ask God to change my attitude and give me the strength, energy, and desire to seek Him. It helps to spend time telling Him who He is to me: "Thank you, Jesus, for being my savior, my provider, my protector."

Then I hear Him saying back to me, "Know that I love you, son. I am pleased with you and you delight Me." Wow! How often I need to hear that!

Dedicated prayer time doesn't guarantee a smooth day will follow. When I first started writing the things God was speaking to me, it all felt clear to me. I would leave my prayer room confident that I would do the things He was telling me to do. That was the easy part. The hard part started when I walked out the door. The issues of the day would hit me, and I would quickly forget what God had told me that morning. After months of that, I was discouraged almost every night when I came home. Then one day I felt like God was telling me not to leave His words in my prayer room, but to make a list of the things I sensed He was telling me or a Bible verse He had led me to, and carry it in my pocket. When I was struggling to believe or obey a word or promise He had given me, I pulled it out of my pocket and read it again.

The words took me back to a posture of prayer and reminded me of what God and I had talked about that morning. I felt that indescribable peace that only God can give us and His strength to do what He was calling me to do.

Now, my prayer every day is, "God, please don't give me more than I can handle ... but don't give me less either. I just want whatever You want."

You need to know that I struggled—and continue to struggle—with my sinful nature and my unwillingness to do what God wants me to do at times. As you will read in the chapters to come, *hearing* God's voice and *heeding* God's voice are two very different things.

4

LEAN YEARS

*M*oving to Waxahachie to go to Bible college turned out to be the beginning of seven years of financial disaster for us—and also a time when we felt God's presence with us, even when we couldn't make things work economically.

That was also about the time that Tracy and I decided to tithe our income to the church. I don't remember a particular event that motivated us, and it was kind of a crazy decision financially. We didn't even have enough money to pay the bills. But we started giving 10 percent of whatever income we had. This isn't a prosperity gospel story. We continued to struggle. But we didn't go hungry (but we also weren't ashamed to call a 59-cent taco and water "dinner"). God fed us and put a roof over our heads.

BUS DRIVERS: THE MOST STRESSFUL JOB EVER

Because I had been successful with the lawn business, I thought I could do something like that, or maybe a house-painting business, while Tracy and I were in college. Moving to Waxahachie didn't worry me at all. It would be a lot of work on top of classes, but no more than when I was in high school, and we would be fine financially. But when we got there, nothing worked. I couldn't get any traction. There were no jobs anywhere.

Tracy and I finally got jobs working for the Waxahachie Independent School District driving buses for kids with disabilities. We were each making about $220 a month.

That was the most stressful job I've ever had. Maybe it was because of my personality; I don't know. They put me in charge of the buses whose drivers had quit because the kids were so out of control. I had to drive the "problem" bus every day for as long as it took to get the kids back under control, and then I could train a new driver and move on to the next one. It was a high-stress job that began to teach me the importance of leading by influence, not by position.

One week, they gave me a bus, and the first morning was crazy. Kids were all over the place, yelling and running. I told them to sit down, but they said they didn't understand English. I dropped them off at school and went inside to ask some questions. Several of the teachers said the kids did all speak English, but some pretended not to understand.

That afternoon when they got on the bus, I called roll. They insisted they did not understand anything I was saying. After several minutes I began to lose patience with their game, so I said, "Let me just explain to you how this works. If your name is not on this sheet, and you don't tell me, then you have to get off this bus and walk home."

Every one of them said, "Yeah, I'm here."

I went home that afternoon thinking I had won. And in the short run, maybe I had. I was able to train a new driver and turn that bus over to him, but I hadn't done anything to help those kids. I hadn't created any meaningful relationship beyond the fact that I was in charge—the definition of influence by position.

In the midst of this stressful job, studying in school, having no money, and being newly married, I began to experience moments when I would suddenly get cold chills, start to sweat, and get dizzy. This started happening every other week and would last a few minutes. Then it started occurring more often and would last a day or more. Over time, it grew to the point that I would start vomiting and slurring my speech. Tracy took me to the emergency room multiple times, and no one could figure out what was wrong. This lasted for close to a year.

Our doctor referred me to a neurosurgeon, and he felt I was either having mini-strokes or possibly had a brain tumor.

Not long after the doctor gave me that diagnosis, I was in the grocery store and somehow started talking to a couple I didn't know. Somehow the subject of my health came up, and these strangers said it sounded like I had something called Meniere's disease and suggested I see an ear, nose, and throat specialist. I had never heard of Meniere's disease; however, since the other options were mini-strokes or a brain tumor, I went as they suggested. In a matter of minutes, the ENT confirmed it was, in fact, Meniere's disease, which is a disorder of the inner ear that can lead to vertigo and hearing loss. He said the disease is often caused by extreme stress and that I would probably have to be on Valium for the rest of my life to deal with it.

Tracy and I went home glad for an answer to the issue. But after trying the Valium for a while, I saw that it sucked the life out of me and made me sleep a lot.

The doctor was right—I was experiencing a lot of stress at work, financially, and in other areas. Tracy and I decided we had to depend on God to fix this, so we started praying for healing, trusting God to deliver. That trust allowed me to release the stress, and after releasing the stress, I have never had another episode, nor have I been on that medication. But it was a wake-up call for me to learn how much I needed to lean on God and not myself.

PRIDE BEFORE A FALL

As we processed how to eliminate more of the stress in our lives and after our first year of college and driving buses, Tracy and I realized we just weren't going to make it financially. After reevaluating our situation, we realized one of us needed to leave school and find a full-time job. After talking it over, we decided I would get my degree first. We both knew there was a good chance I'd never get back to school if I started my career first. Tracy got a job at VarTec Telecom in Lancaster, so at least one of us wasn't driving a bus every morning and afternoon. Since we had only one vehicle—a little Toyota truck with a stick shift and no air conditioning—I had to take her to work and pick her up every day.

My morning started at 4:30 a.m., when I got up to drive the bus. After I finished my run, I picked Tracy up and took her to work. Then I rushed to my first class at 8:00 a.m. and had classes almost all day. At 2:30 p.m., I drove back to the bus barn and started my afternoon rounds, getting the kids home. Finally, I drove the truck back to Lancaster to pick up Tracy and studied while she fixed supper.

I got so frustrated with the time I was wasting shuttling Tracy to and from work because we only had the one car, and she couldn't even drive it (she couldn't drive a stick shift). Baking inside the truck from the Texas heat only made things worse. I told Tracy we were going to get a new truck. "We're just going to trust God that if we qualify for credit, He'll help us pay for it."

That Saturday, we drove to the Ford dealership and picked out a truck with automatic transmission and air conditioning (praise God!). We filled out the credit application, and the credit manager came out of his office a few minutes later.

"I just wanted to come out here and meet you," he said. "I've never met anybody so young with a credit score as high as yours."

I could feel my chest swelling with pride as he went on, because even though we didn't have much money, all those years in business had given me great credit.

You probably think it doesn't make sense for a college student who drives a school bus to have a such a great credit score. But I had been on my own for seven years and had managed my brother's and my business debt well, and Tracy and I hadn't taken on any additional debt.

As the credit manager spoke, I thought about my parents, who had declared bankruptcy. But instead of feeling grateful for the sacrifices they had made for me and my siblings, I thought that I must be a lot smarter than they were because of my credit score.

God had a plan to deal with my pride. In the meantime, though, Tracy and I were smart enough *not* to buy that truck. We went home from the dealership, prayed about it, and then followed God's lead to a wiser decision: hold off on buying a new vehicle and buy a small used car instead.

TRUTH AND REVELATION

Sometimes I think I know so much of the Word of God that I don't even see the truth right in front of me.

There's a story in the Bible about a Pharisee named Nicodemus who goes to Jesus one night to ask about His teaching.

Jesus says, "You are Israel's teacher . . . and do you not understand these things?" (John 3:10).

Nicodemus was supposed to be one of the most respected religious leaders, and yet he didn't understand.

As I grew in my knowledge of the Bible, I became so embedded in what I *thought* I knew that I didn't see what God was trying to tell me. God began to challenge me to read and listen with my *heart*—not just with my eyes and brain.

He will reveal truth to us when we humble ourselves before Him and open our hearts and minds to hear it. I began to seek the Lord in a deeper way, and He quickly revealed things to me—like how I needed His help to control my temper, which had always been a problem.

I spent almost all my time as a kid with my brother and, when his friends made me mad, I challenged them to fights. They were four years older than me, so it was easy for them to walk away. They didn't want to beat up a little kid.

Mike and my dad have told me that, when I was really young, I would sometimes threaten to hit people with a baseball bat. I don't remember that, but I believe them.

Shortly after our parents divorced, Mike and I were at home one night with Dad sitting on the sofa watching TV when somebody suddenly kicked the front door in. We all jumped up, not knowing what was going on. Before we could react, the intruder charged at my dad, and they began fighting right there in the living room. I recognized the guy as someone we knew from church, and I only learned later why he was so angry at my dad. I'll skip *those* details.

At that point, all we knew was someone had busted into our house and attacked our dad. My father always kept a loaded .357 Magnum revolver in a drawer in the living room. Mike and I ran for it at the same time, neither of us afraid to use a gun. The revolver wasn't there, though, so we ran back to where we kept the rest of the guns, and Mike started loading. By the time we got back to the living room, the other man had run out the front door and was driving away.

A couple of weeks later, Dad told us he had moved the .357 out of the drawer the night before that incident. I believe the Holy Spirit had nudged him to do that. I've thought about that night many times—how our lives would look completely different if he hadn't moved that revolver and one of us had used it in anger or revenge. I can look back and see God's protection upon my life.

Years later, I was in high school when Dad did something—I don't remember what—that made me so mad I went to confront him. By then, Dad was a manager with an office in Fort Worth, and I drove out there and stormed into his office. I started yelling at him, but he stayed calm.

Dad had a temper, too, and I knew that. I knew he would respond to my anger with his own. And when I challenged him to fight me, I knew he would.

But he didn't. He just said, "Son, that's not going to help."

His response frustrated me. If he wouldn't fight, all I could do was walk away. It wasn't long before I realized how wise he had been and how dumb I had been.

I carried my temper into my adult years. Tracy and I hadn't been married long, and we would drive back and forth from Waxahachie to Waco every Sunday and Wednesday night to work with the youth group. Driving up and down I-35, if a car was tailing me too closely, I would tap the brakes and make them back off. If they didn't, I'd hit the brakes *hard*. I was carrying a lot of anger. Fortunately, nobody rear-ended me.

One afternoon when I did that, the car behind me swerved to keep from hitting us. I got off at the next exit to go to a store, and that same car followed me into the parking lot. I thought the driver might be looking for a fight, and I was ready. He opened the door and got out, and every muscle in my body tightened up in anticipation. Then, the other doors of his car opened and three little kids got out. They all went inside—a happy family just doing some shopping.

I was so stupid. I was also convicted. I could have killed that man and his children on the highway. I had to change. I needed God's help.

But then, something else happened that pushed my anger to the limits.

My brother and his wife were thinking of moving to Midlothian, and they lived with Tracy and me for a while. I came home one day to find my brother, father, and wife sitting in the living room, with Tracy in tears. It was obvious somebody had said something that had upset her badly.

I said, "What the heck's going on?"

Nobody would answer, and that created an opportunity for my temper to really get going. Eventually, I figured out that my brother had said something hurtful, and I told him I was going to whip him right then and there. Dad stepped in to try to calm things down, and I told him I'd whip him too.

This was after I'd finished Bible college. After I had learned to pray and listen to God. After I had been married for several years and had a young son. After years of working with the youth in our church. And after I had been sharing the Gospel with my family for years!

Neither of them would fight me, and after a while, they just left. That's when it hit me: they would never see me as a man of God if I kept acting that way. If I was ever going to really impact my family for Christ, I had to change. I couldn't just *tell them* how much God was changing me; I had to *show them*. I had to walk it out. They had to see me change.

I prayed and asked God again to help me with my temper and attitude, and I kept praying for a long time. I wanted Him to really search my heart. Change comes slowly. Even now, I know certain things will trigger my temper. I can feel it rising inside of me, and I've mostly learned to take myself out of those situations immediately. Mostly.

The apostle Paul wrote, "I want to do what is good, but I don't. I don't want to do what is wrong, but I do it anyway.... What a miserable person I am!" (Romans 7:19, 24a, NLT).

But there is hope for Paul, for me, and for you: "Who will free me from this life that is dominated by sin and death? Thank God! The answer is in Christ Jesus our Lord." (Romans 24b–25, NLT).

God has taught me to walk away, and he's given me the strength to do it. I don't want to be that old person again. If a contractor, supplier, or customer starts to push me to a place where I know I might lose my temper, I give in before I argue. The confrontation is not worth it. I am still learning how not to give in to my natural reaction. I ask God to help me understand what is really going on. Why did I lose my temper in the first place? What is the root cause? I refuse to believe the lie that my temper is just who I am or that I was simply born this way. I *can* change. God *is* changing me and helping me become more like Him.

A HARD LESSON IN RESPECT

In high school I had been so proud of my independence. I'd go to the grocery store to buy my own groceries and see a guy older than me bagging groceries, and I'd think, *Dude, I will never sack groceries. I can make a whole lot more money doing yards and building a business.*

That's an example of how I thought I was better, smarter, and more successful than others. But I didn't love, value, or respect other people, nor did I have patience for them. For example, Tracy and I were at a restaurant one night, and I asked our waitress for some sweetener for my tea. After a few minutes, she hadn't brought any, so I asked her again.

Impatiently, I asked Tracy, "How hard is it to bring me what I asked for? It ain't rocket science, you know."

Our waitress walked past our table empty-handed again, and I called her over and said, "I don't understand how hard it is to get us a little sweetener. Do you want me to go get it for you?"

A minute later, she came back with an apron full of pink packets and dumped them on the table. I mean, a pile of those things. She didn't say a word. She just turned around and walked off.

I shrugged and asked Tracy, "What was that about?"

Just then, the manager came out, apologized to us, and picked up the packets. "Man, I don't know what happened to her," he said, "but she just quit."

"She quit?" I said, feeling a sudden punch in the gut.

"Yeah, she quit. I can't believe she did it. I mean, she's got a baby at home and she's a single mom, and she quit. I honestly don't know how she is going to make it."

I felt awful and immediately wanted to find her and apologize. Maybe there was something else going on with her, but obviously my disrespect had pushed her to quit a job she needed.

You never know what other people are going through—the waitress at your table, the guy doing a job you feel you are too good, too smart, or too successful to do. God needed to humble me and show me how my temper and disrespect for others had an impact. And He did just that in multiple ways.

MY MOTHER SHOWS ME I
NEED A NEW HEART

The Lord never ceases to amaze me in how He works, even when I don't get it. He did so much for so long to get ahold of my heart, attitude, and perspective, which were wrong in so many ways, as you have probably figured out.

God used my mother to open my eyes to more places in my heart that He wanted to deal with: my disrespect for the one I loved most in this world.

Nearly two years into my marriage, Mom visited from Tennessee and stayed with us at our duplex. One afternoon, she said she needed a smoke. She'd been smoking all my life, sometimes lighting the next one with the one she was finishing, so she'd literally be holding two cigarettes at once. I had asked her not to smoke in the house and she always respected us and stepped out.

"Will you come out here with me?" she asked, walking toward the front door.

I followed her out to our tiny front porch and, after I closed the door and we sat down, she said, "Johnny, you know I love you, right?"

"Yes, ma'am," I said.

"You know your father and I were married almost twenty years, and you guys never really saw us fight."

"Yes."

She continued, "I can tell you from being married almost twenty years that someone being harsh, putting you down, and telling jokes at your expense—it gets old over time."

I began to remember. My mother was submissive to my father. That's the model I saw growing up. Men led the household, women submitted. At family reunions, my grandmother, my great-grandmother, and all my aunts would work in the kitchen for hours preparing a meal and then serving it to the men. When the men finished eating, the women sat down to eat before cleaning up.

My father was in charge of our home, and my mother submitted to him. He went out and earned a living. She cooked the meals, cleaned the house, and washed the clothes. My brother and I did yard work. I honestly don't ever remember not working. From as early as I can remember, my brother and I cut the grass, raked leaves, and did whatever our parents told us to do. It all made sense to me. That's the way the world worked.

Tracy and I didn't argue either. She had always been quiet, even shy. It was understood that if she did what I said, everything would be fine. The man was the spiritual leader of the household, and he was the dominant figure—that was the way I thought it always worked. (Don't throw the book away! I am going somewhere with this. This was my old heart, not my new heart.)

Mom lit a cigarette and inhaled, and our porch filled with that familiar smell of burning tobacco. I wondered why we were having this conversation. Then she looked at me and said, "Johnny, you don't understand how you're talking to Tracy, but I see how you're treating her. You're not respecting her. And to her, it might not seem like a big deal today. But in fifteen or twenty years, it's going to be a huge deal. She's going to get tired of it."

Me? My first thought was to defend myself. *What had I done? What had I said?* But then, in an instant, I knew she was right. I was treating Tracy just like Dad had treated Mom, the way his father had treated his mother, the way I had seen so many men treat women. I saw a picture of Tracy and me in our future, and it was just like my mother described it. Their marriage had not survived. Would ours?

"You have to love and respect Tracy for who she is," Mom said.

The conversation was over before she lit her second cigarette, but those were some of the most significant words she ever spoke to me. I asked God to change my heart. I couldn't do it alone. I didn't even know where to start or how I should act.

God began working on me immediately, jabbing my conscience whenever I was harsh with Tracy and showing me what it meant to be a servant leader. I had to seek God and His love first, and only then serve my family. I needed to really understand how Christ loved me so I could follow His example and love Tracy like that.

That talk with my mother was more than twenty-five years ago, and I still ask God every day to transform my heart and mind and to change the way I think and behave to reflect Him and His character. The new heart He is giving me affects every relationship with every person in my life.

LOSING MY MOM

Following God's instructions has not always been easy. Not long after my porch conversation with Mom, she decided to move back to Texas. Her alcoholism and depression seemed to be getting worse. She would call me more often and say she was going to kill herself, and I was able to calm her down each time.

One morning toward the end of my second year at college, I was praying and wrote a note in my journal that I should ask Mom to forgive me. Well, that didn't make any sense. Why would I need to ask her to forgive me? I thought I had been helping her and offering her support for years. But the Lord kept on telling me, "You need to ask her to forgive you for the way you've thought about her, the way you've talked to her, and the way you've talked about her."

I knew He was right, but I pushed back. I just didn't want to do it. I kept thinking, *Why should I apologize when she and Dad were the ones who left me?* That went on for two weeks each morning during my prayer time and even throughout the day. Finally, one Saturday morning, I felt Him deep in my spirit saying, "John, you need to do this *today*."

I decided to go see her, but I prayed, "God, you're going to have to help me, because this is hard, and I don't want to."

Tracy and I drove to Mom's apartment in Irving that afternoon, and I thought about the words I needed to say. Reminding her of specific examples might hurt her even more. God's purpose was for me to apologize and express my love and respect. We got there, and I told Mom I was sorry for things I had said to her and said about her through the years. I told her how much I loved her and how I was glad she had moved back to Texas so we could spend more time together. Then I asked her to forgive me.

She smiled and said, "Johnny, I sure love you and yes, I forgive you. Will you forgive me as well?"

"Of course," I said.

I felt a weight lifting off me—something I hadn't expected. Mom, Tracy, and I enjoyed a conversation that was filled with hope for the future.

Then she said, "You know, maybe it's time for me to get my life right with the Lord. I'm sick this weekend or I would go to church with you tomorrow, but can I go with you next Sunday?"

"Sure," I said. "We'd love that."

We were all excited for Mom and this new chapter. She needed God's strength to rebuild her life. Plus, our church could help her find structure, support, and a place of purpose. Then, the very next Monday night, about 1:30 a.m., the phone rang. It was Mom. She'd been drinking and she was crying. She started talking about her past, her pain, and how much she was suffering. "Johnny," she sobbed, "I'm just going to kill myself."

I was so disappointed because I had believed she might be making a turn. This was the same pattern she'd followed for more than ten years. Her addiction to alcohol was so powerful, it was going to take a lot more than one afternoon with Tracy and me to give her strength to break it.

In the middle of the night, I didn't know what else I could do for her. I listened to her, then I said, "I love you, Mom, and I'll talk to you tomorrow."

But I never spoke to her again. After we hung up, my mother took a handful of pills and overdosed. She was gone.

When somebody in your life commits suicide, people come and take the body away, and the survivors are left alone. There's nobody else to clean up literally, financially, and emotionally. So while my brother and I were dealing with our grief and our guilt, we were also picking up the pieces our mother left behind.

I went to my professors and explained what had happened. "I have no idea how long this is going to take because I have never been in this situation before," I said.

My business professors said, "You go do whatever you need to do, and when you get back, we'll figure out school. Take however long you need."

But a Bible professor told me, "Man, I'm sorry for your loss, but don't forget if you miss more than two classes, you need to drop the class."

That really ticked me off. Where was the grace he was teaching us about in his class?

Then a couple of people I had known my whole life and some I even went to church with told me how sad they were that my mom had committed suicide— because it meant she was going to hell.

I thought, *Who are these people?* Are these professors and people from church actually representing God?

I turned my frustration toward Him: "You're the God who let my mom get to the finish line—my mom who literally said it was time to get her life right with the Lord. And now these people who supposedly love You and follow You and teach Your Word to express Your love say You have sent her to hell because she took her own life? If that's who You are and that's who they are, then I don't want to follow You. I don't want anything to do with You."

And so, I walked away from God. I decided I was going to finish school because we had loans to repay and I needed a degree. But we stopped going to church, stopped tithing, and stopped having anything to do with God. When we were at Tracy's parents' house, they would ask us to go to church with them, but we never did.

Finally, after about a year, I gave in and told Tracy, "Fine, I will go if it will get your parents to stop asking. But I'm telling you, I'm sitting in the back and I am leaving when it's over."

I don't remember anything about the service that day or what the preacher said. I do remember God getting ahold of my heart and saying, "Son, I love you, and I've given you a time to mourn. Now it's time for you to make a decision about whether you're going to follow Me or not."

God gave me the peace to know that, sometimes, all I can do is trust Him and know I may not always understand, but I *can* be confident that He was with my mom and He was with me.

I said, "Okay, yeah, I'm all in," and I decided to *fully* follow Christ that day.

A true healing began in my heart, and I started to understand God's love more than if I hadn't have gone through that process. I was reminded of the passage that says, "Give thanks in all circumstances; for this is God's will for you in Christ Jesus" (1 Thessalonians 5:18).

How could I give God thanks for my mom's suicide? Well, I didn't thank Him that she took her life, but I thanked Him for being with me through the process and for being with Mom. My perception of Him is different than it was before.

So I wasn't thanking Him because of the terrible situation I was in, but because of who He is. He is faithful to His Word, which is truth, and He brought revelation through those difficult times.

Coming out the other side of it, I realized I had never really known the character of God, so I didn't know Him personally. I had not understood the depth

of the true love He has for me and won't fully understand until I am in heaven with Him. There was a side
of God and His personality that I had never experienced. It was at that point that the Lord really started
dealing with my heart, telling me, "There's been so
much hardness in your heart because of how you have
perceived the way people treated you. Now you have
a decision to make: you can keep living the way you
have before, or you can choose to represent Me the way
I'm showing you, which means you will be expressing
much more love, grace, mercy, and empathy."

Years later, I still struggle to demonstrate those qual-
ities at times, but that's when God gives me opportunities to make a difference. Christians can sometimes be
the hardest, most critical people to know, work with,
or work for. I can't count the times somebody has told
me, "I thought you were a believer," or, "I thought you
were a Christian" when they didn't agree with something I said or a business decision I made.

I *am* a Christian, but the reality is we're not perfect.
We all fall short of the glory of God, and everything
we do is going to have flaws. And even when we do
everything right, there will be people who accuse of
acting ungodly. At the end of the day, the best we can

do is follow Christ as closely as possible, knowing we can never do that with perfection.

FOLLOWING AN EARTHLY MODEL

In my first three years of college, we had a hard time getting plugged into a church near school, so we stayed involved at our home church in Waco. Driving down every Wednesday night was sort of a hassle—about eighty miles each way—and we didn't understand why God wasn't opening doors for us closer to our new home. But we loved the youth group kids in Waco, and God gave us signs that He was with us. Like the Wednesday night we left home with less than a quarter tank of gas in the truck and not a dime in our pockets. Nothing under the sofa cushions, nothing anywhere, and two days until payday.

After church, we hung around a little longer than usual waiting for somebody to ask, "Need anything?" We trusted God would nudge somebody's heart to give us $20 or so for gas to get back home, but nobody spoke up. So we got back in the truck and headed north on I-35. I watched the needle more than the road as it crept toward E and then dropped below. Maybe God would send us help on the side of the road when we ran out of gas. Incredibly, though, we made it all the way home, and I breathed a huge sigh of relief when I turned off the ignition. But we still didn't have gas, and payday was Friday.

Over the next two days, I never ran out of gas. I literally drove around town for two days and one night with my fuel gage on empty, and I know without a doubt that this was a miracle. This was such a big deal to me because I knew God was helping us and teaching us how to trust Him with every single situation. So often, God reminds us He is with us even in the little things. The real question is, do we recognize it? You can bet I told that story everywhere I went, especially the next Wednesday night at church.

Danny Kent's children were members of the Waco youth group, so I stayed in touch with Danny and his wife, Maggie. Danny was the man who had stood at the church door when I was a kid and invited me to sit with him and his family. In the summer after my sophomore year at Bible college, Tracy and I didn't have school buses to drive, so I needed to find work.

Danny offered me a job doing plumbing. I had never accepted his invitation to sit with them at church as a kid, but I did accept this one. Over time, his model as a man, a husband, a father, and as a leader made a huge impact on the person I have become.

Before that summer, I only knew Danny as twelve-year-old Daniel's dad. He loved Jesus, but he wasn't a guy who carried his Bible around everywhere. Rather, I knew he loved Jesus because of the way he carried himself and treated people.

I saw that model all summer long. He never yelled and screamed at subcontractors or the people who worked for him when things went wrong. He incorporated Christ into his daily life and in everything he was doing. Through it all, he was very successful in his business.

I saw how he met the needs of people at work and, by watching him with his wife and children, I saw how he treated his family. He was the same man at work, church, and home. Tracy and I grew closer to his family, and Danny became a mentor to me.

One morning about two weeks after school started and we were back into our routine in Waxahachie, Maggie called me. Danny had gotten up early—he always got up around 4:30 a.m.—sat on the edge of the bed and said, "Maggie, I just want you to know how much I love you and how blessed I am to be your husband." He leaned over and kissed her, stood up, and then slumped over and fell to the floor. They didn't realize he had heart disease, and he had a massive heart attack that morning. By the time the ambulance arrived, it was too late.

At his funeral, I began to see the impact he had on so many people, and Maggie received cards and letters for months from people telling her how Danny had helped people in ways he had never mentioned— quietly serving as Christ's hands and feet in the world. He loved people where they were.

For a while after Danny died, Daniel didn't want to talk to anyone about his father. I was honored a little later when he told his mom he wanted to talk to me. He knew I had recently lost my mom, and he knew how much I loved his father. So I drove down and spent as much time as I could with him, answering questions about his dad. He wanted to know everything I could tell him—the stories, the lessons, everything.

Danny had poured so much into him, but now he was gone, and I wanted to do for Daniel what Danny had done for me. I also loved Daniel very much (still do) and saw so much of his dad in him even at twelve years old. I was still young myself and definitely didn't show him that love as well as his father had. But I tried to be the example his dad had modeled for me.

God was revealing to me how He can use us to touch the people He loves if we will just do the little things He asks us to do. We're not going to get it right every time, but we can press on growing and becoming more like Christ daily to become better imitators of Him.

Years ago, when I felt so alone, Danny had asked me to sit with his family in church. That one small act made a real difference back then. And it still impacts my life today.

5

LEARNING GOD'S
ECONOMICS

*E*ven though we were broke and I was still in college, Tracy and I felt like God was telling us to build a house. We had no idea how that could ever happen.

"God, we don't have any money and don't have enough income coming in each month to pay a house payment," we said. "Don't You understand how this works? It doesn't make sense for us to try to build a house right now."

Yet we both felt God saying, "Yeah, but I'm telling you to do this anyway."

The U.S. Department of Agriculture had a mortgage program for rural development that was available in Midlothian, about ten miles from campus. They even subsidized the mortgage payment. We filled out an application and were a little more optimistic because, even though we didn't have much income, we had no debt. And hey, I had a great credit score, remember?

The process was long, and we went through almost a year of praying and waiting before they ever contacted us. When we went in for a personal interview and the loan officer looked at our application, he started laughing right in front of us.

He looked at our total income, which was basically nothing, then looked up and asked, "Is this a joke?"

He had a dip of snuff under his front lip and reached for a little cup to spit into.

"No sir," I said. "This isn't a joke."

"What are you thinking, applying for this?" he said.

"We honestly believe this is what God told us to do," I explained, "and we're just trying to be faithful to the process."

"Okay," he said, "I can tell you that this isn't going to happen. There is no way I'm approving this loan."

"What do we have to do to appeal this decision?" I asked.

"Well, you submit your appeal to me, and I don't see that happening."

He went ahead and told us the process and gave us the papers we needed to file an appeal. On the way out of the office, his assistant told us to keep in touch with her if we thought she could help us in any way.

The appeal had to be decided in sixty days or we would have to start the process over from the beginning, so we submitted our paperwork right away. Then we waited. When we didn't hear anything after a few weeks, so we tried to schedule an appointment.

However, the man making the decision would never put us back on his calendar.

Then, literally the day of the deadline, I called again. His assistant answered and said, "What can I do for you today?"

I said, "We really need to get on his calendar because our time is up tomorrow."

"Consider it done," she said. "You can come in tomorrow."

We walked in the next day, and he put down his little spit cup and said, "Let me tell you, I don't know why we're doing this. The numbers don't make sense whatsoever. But I have decided to give you a loan for a house."

He slid a sheet of paper across his desk and, based on our income, showed us that our monthly payment would be $176 a month. No down payment.

We were shocked at the low monthly payment. We were already paying $275 a month rent.

"Is this for real?" I asked.

"That's it," he said.

We never fully understood what happened, except to know that he had followed the regulations and our low income, plus the blessing and favor of the Lord, was the only explanation. The house would be small but felt huge to us, because it was twice the size of our duplex. More importantly, it would be ours. Then Tracy's dad found a clause where the U.S.D.A. said the homes in this program should meet the minimum size requirements of local building codes. Midlothian's minimum for this subdivision was 1,100 square feet and a few other requirements, so our house would have three bedrooms, two bathrooms, and a two-car garage. There were also optional upgrades, but we couldn't afford any of them.

We started the process of building our first house and met with a builder who worked with this government program. They provided the construction loan and then converted it to a mortgage at closing. If we stayed in the house for seven years, the equity was ours to keep.

LEARNING GOD'S ECONOMICS

After Mom died and I later fully rededicated my life to the Lord, we began paying our tithe again, and I started to understand God's economics. It didn't make any sense, but we were getting a new home for almost $100 a month *less* than our rent. Even then we felt like we were barely getting by. We didn't buy extras like cable TV.

Before long, God started challenging us in our giving. I was standing in the checkout line at the grocery store the first time God asked me to give above and beyond our tithe. A woman pushed her cart in behind me, and I felt Him saying to me, "I want you to buy that woman's groceries."

I looked back out of the corner of my eye, and I thought, "Dude, she's got way more money than I do. She doesn't need my money."

And the Lord spoke to me and said, "You're right. She doesn't need the money, but she needs to know I love her."

How do you argue with that? I couldn't. I knew I only had $13, so I was hoping she wasn't buying more than that. She didn't.

I honestly don't remember her reaction, but I do know that was the first time I stepped out in faith to obey God with my money. Once again, God was giving me opportunities to share His love by doing one little thing. I was simply the conduit between Him and someone else, and the experience changed my heart.

A few weeks later, we completed our tax return and realized we were getting a $500 refund. We were excited because we had not had extra money for so long, and we started making plans for what we could do with it. In those days, $500 felt like $100,000.

We decided to spend some of it on a trip—stay in a hotel for couple of nights, go out to eat, and catch a couple of movies. We'd still have money left to put away when we got home.

At church that Sunday, though, I felt the Lord speak to me. "See that lady sitting behind you? She really needs that $500."

I thought that couldn't be right—and I sure wanted to go on that trip. Was I hearing my own thoughts and not God's voice? But He continued.

"Trust Me," He said. "I'm taking you somewhere with this. I just want you to trust Me. She really needs that money."

I leaned over and whispered to Tracy, "I think God's telling me to give the $500 we just got to the lady behind us."

Without hesitating, Tracy said, "I think you're right."

When the service ended, we introduced ourselves to the woman and explained what we had heard from God. The lady cried when Tracy wrote a check for $500. She said her family had a medical bill for almost exactly that, and they didn't know how they were going to pay it.

God was teaching us to trust Him in larger ways. Even though we were still living paycheck to paycheck and had no extra money, we had such a joy and peace in our hearts that God was doing something in us and through us.

I thought about the people in my life who had shared the love of Jesus with me. Where would I be, for example, if Danny Kent hadn't stood at the door of the church all those Sundays? What if he hadn't offered me a job that summer when he showed me how a servant leader operates his business?

I believe a gift of $500 or $13—when God is using that gift—can totally change the trajectory of someone's life for eternity, including your own.

OPENING OUR DOORS

When the builders finished our new house and we moved in, it was one of the most humbling experiences ever. Moving from that little duplex, where I had fallen through the ceiling and where we struggled to keep warm on winter nights, into our own brand-new home on a beautiful corner lot was an incredible gift from God.

Tracy and I quickly realized this wonderful gift wasn't just for us, just as the $13 and the $500 weren't only for us. We began to feel the Lord laying it on our hearts to open our home to let other people live with us. We started praying for Him to show us who. It wasn't long before we had two young men living with us. The Master's Commission program at our church trained young people for pastoral work, and they needed a place to live while they were going through the program.

The parents of one of the boys living with us had divorced, and his situation reminded me a lot of my own. Tracy and I had a real heart for him, and he lived with us for four years.

We took them in and loved on them the best we knew how. We didn't really know what we were doing, but I remembered from my Bible class the commission to "Go and make disciples." So we tried to share with them what we were learning about Christ, marriage, building a family, and money—because we still didn't have any extra, and finances were even tighter with two eighteen-year-old young men in the house. Let's just say they got their fair share of frozen pizzas and mac and cheese.

Over the years, the Lord has continued to use us that way. We've had more than fifty people live with us at different times. It's been crazy to watch the Lord bring the right ones at the right time. So many of them came from broken homes and had never seen a good marriage or a healthy family. Tracy and I tried to be real and open about all the things God was trying to change in us, in our marriage, in our finances, in our walks with Him, and many other areas.

Each step of the way, God was faithful. We are not perfect by any means, and I know all those young people could tell you that, but we still have relationships with almost all of them, their spouses, and their children. It's truly like we have kids all over America. Some are businesspeople, some teachers, some pastors. It has been a blessing that we almost missed because we thought this was *our* house and we wanted to just live in it, relax, and enjoy it. But God had a better plan for the house that was beyond us. He made that house a true home for us and so many others.

THE CRASH

Soon after we were settled in our new home, Tracy got an hourly job in Dallas and was driving back and forth to work every day. One morning while driving to work, a truck rear-ended her and totaled the car. The wreck was so bad, the Dallas policeman who brought her home said that he'd seen a lot of accidents on the same bridge in his twenty years on the force, but he'd never seen a car stay on the bridge after it had been hit as hard as Tracy's. All the others were pushed off the bridge, and the drivers were killed.

She didn't go to the hospital, despite the officer's insistence, but she needed a lot of physical therapy. She went five days a week for three months and couldn't go to work that entire time. The insurance companies got into an argument over who was at fault, the truck that rear-ended Tracy or a car that forced the truck into Tracy's lane. The driver of that other car had driven away, and the trucker's insurance refused to pay. Our insurance company had to step in.

We had bought Tracy's car used and couldn't afford to carry collision insurance, so we didn't get anything for that. Our insurance paid for some, but not all, of the ninety physical therapy sessions Tracy needed to get back to full strength. And the company she worked for didn't pay her during her absence because she had only been on the job a couple months.

With higher expenses and lower income, we relied on credit cards to bridge the gap. For months, we could barely make the minimum payment. Suddenly, for the first time in our lives, we were deeply in debt. And yet I was still cocky about our situation. My parents had filed for bankruptcy, and I was determined that I wouldn't. My credit was so strong and my ability to work through a crisis was so focused, I was sure we would be fine. I was confident I could press through, work hard, and figure it out.

Tracy went back to work four months after the accident, but we couldn't keep up with all the payments. A year later, we worked with a debt consolidation program, but we still couldn't catch up. Our only choice was to declare bankruptcy. I still hadn't realized it, but I had made an idol of my great credit score and my confidence in making things happen. Then everything came crashing down on us.

I will always give my parents the credit for instilling a strong work ethic in my siblings and me. So even in bankruptcy, I believed I could accomplish whatever I needed to do. We had lost everything except our house and our other car. We were broke; despite that, my spirit wasn't broken because I knew I was a child of God.

UNDERSTANDING GOD'S CALL FOR MY LIFE

I was still in college, we were trying to pay the bills and deal with the aftermath of bankruptcy, and I was figuring out what I would do after I graduated. I was getting a business degree, but the school encouraged me to go into church administration, adding to my confusion about what to do. Should I work in the church or the business world? Professors, counselors, and other students said, "God didn't call you to go to Bible college if He wanted you out in the business world. If you're in Bible college, you must be called to full-time ministry." That confused me. In their minds, that meant a career within the four walls of a church.

Many of them told me that people were not "called" to the business world. Yet I had the stirring in me to go into secular business, and I believed that's where God wanted me to work. I loved the church, but I couldn't see myself working in that world every day.

Tracy's brother, Troy, had an internship at Oak Cliff Assembly of God church in Red Oak and was in a discipleship program led by Scott Wilson, the youth pastor. Troy suggested I meet with Scott and see what he said. We had lunch at a Whataburger, and I poured my heart out to him saying, "I'm just trying to figure out what God wants me to do."

Scott listened to me patiently, then he said, "You just need to pray about it and do whatever God tells you to do. You need to do that every day."

Well, that answer ticked me off because I needed a decision, and I wanted Scott to tell me what to do—to make it clear to me. It's always easier to seek wise counsel and have somebody tell me what to do than it is to actually go to my prayer closet, spend time seeking the Lord for the answer, and then walk it out faithfully. But Scott didn't give me the answer. So I prayed, and day by day I felt even stronger that God was calling me to work in the business world.

A BABY, A FULL HOUSE, A WRECK, AND FINANCIAL DISASTER

We had been married for about four years when Tracy said it was time to think about having a baby. Well, that really didn't make sense to me. I was still in college, about to graduate, and I didn't have any money or a good-paying job. A baby? Then in my prayer time, I felt God saying, "Dude, it's time for you to get over yourself. You've gotten too set in your ways. It's time for you guys to have a baby." Again, this made no sense to me, and I had no idea how I was supposed to pay for having the baby or raising a child. The Lord simply said, "Trust me."

About halfway through my senior year, I had a couple of offers to work in church administration after I graduated. They both sounded good, and we could have used the money, but I still didn't feel God calling me to make my career in the church. I had to turn them down.

Everything changed when Tracy got pregnant. Of course, I was excited that God was giving us a child, but I also felt even more pressure to get a job to help take care of my growing family. We continued to pray, and I sent out résumés and kept interviewing.

I was offered a job at the Annuity Board of the Southern Baptist Convention—working with retirement accounts, not church work—in 1997 when Tracy was three months pregnant. The Annuity Board's employee insurance would accept all preexisting conditions, including pregnancy.

God was telling us, "See, I've got you covered."

I took the job, and then Tracy got back on her college track. She enrolled at the University of Texas at Arlington studying information technology through her pregnancy. She was taking a ton of hours so she could finish and start her career.

Our son, Austin, was born in 1998, and we brought him home to our little house, where we still had two other young men living with us. So in that 1,100-square-foot house, we had Tracy, me, two young men, and Austin.

It was winter break when Austin was born, and Tracy went back to school when classes started up again. Tracy's mom kept Austin, which was a big blessing for us. He had some issues with his stomach and had to be on the most expensive ready-to-feed baby formula you could buy. Tracy and I started cleaning some warehouses five nights a week on top of my job at the Annuity Board and her schoolwork just to cover diapers and formula. God opened doors for us, but we had to be willing to seize the opportunity and work hard.

6

CHANGES, PAIN, AND GROWTH

I had been working at the Annuity Board for almost two years when a job opening came up that would be a promotion and pay raise for me in the compliance department. I applied for the job and got it, and for the first time in my life I was able to work normal hours, managing the department budget and serving as a liaison between the legal and compliance department and information technology. Anytime the systems were updated, my job was to manage the transition.

For the first few days, Tracy and I praised God for the opportunity—the door He had opened for us.

Then, during my second week, I went to a work conference in Birmingham, Alabama, and realized I was in the wrong place. I'm an outdoors guy. I like hunting and fishing. I cut grass for a living for years, and I loved it.

One of my least-favorite things in the world is technology, and on the first day of the conference, I was surrounded by people talking about systems, coding, software . . . all kinds of craziness (at least that was what it sounded like to me). Computers were their world, and they wouldn't have it any other way. I couldn't believe I had accepted this new job.

I called Tracy that night and said, "I don't know what I've gotten myself into. If this is what the job is all about, there is no way I can do it. I can't listen to and work on this stuff all day. I hate IT!" Tracy could relate . . . but not to me. She was on Team IT because she was finishing up her degree in information technology!

That night, I went to my knees in the hotel room and asked God why in the world He put me in that position. I felt Him responding, "Son, if I put you in this job for five years and one person comes to know me, is it worth it?"

My response was quick. "No," I said out loud.

I immediately knew that was the wrong answer. "But it's the truth," I said. "You know that."

God's response was to begin showing me that I still had a major heart problem. I wanted to be a person who believed that leading a single person to Him was worth five years of a job I didn't like, but in my heart, I wasn't there. So God was taking me completely out of my comfort zone, making me interact with people I never would've interacted with, and having me learn processes and systems that I never would have before.

Here's the crazy part: without those years of experience in helping manage a large budget and diving into systems and operations, I would not have had the ability to run a large, complex business. So not only was the Lord working on my heart, He was also preparing me for the next step in my career. He put me exactly where I needed to be when I needed to be there—not just for me but for the one (or the many) I could influence for Him.

OUR NEW CHURCH HOME

Another place God put us was at Oak Cliff Assembly of God, where Tracy's brother, Troy, had interned and introduced me to Scott Wilson, the youth pastor. Rev. Tom Wilson, Scott's father, had been the senior pastor at Oak Cliff for about a decade and had turned around a church in decline by responding to the changing community.

A decade before Rev. Wilson was called to Oak Cliff, Sunday attendance averaged around fifteen hundred. But in the 1980s, the Red Oak community outside the church had become much more diverse. The church—virtually all white—did not change with the times, however, and weekly attendance fell to fewer than two hundred fifty as families moved out of the community.

Tom Wilson had been leading a much larger church in Austin but was intrigued when Oak Cliff called. Oak Cliff Assembly of God had a long and important history. Oral Roberts had held his first Dallas revivals at the church. The Voice of Healing movement and Christ for the Nations had their beginnings with the people of Oak Cliff. And Pastor H.C. Noah, who served there for thirty-eight years, broadcast the *Morning Worship Hour* on the radio for decades. Tom Wilson's wife had grown up listening to Pastor Noah. "So there was such a history there and such an anointing there," Scott Wilson says, "I think that provided some of the draw for my father. The Lord was saying there's a lot more that I want to do in this place."

Tom Wilson also had a vision for a multicultural church—a reconciliation church where Blacks, Hispanics, Whites, and others would worship God together.

All those things led him to respond to the call to Oak Cliff. They also aligned with Troy's heart when he interned there. They aligned with our hearts as well.

We began to consider moving our church member-
ship from Waco.

LOSING TROY

After his internship at Oak Cliff, Troy was a youth
pastor at the same church in Waco where we had all
grown up, as well as at another church just outside of
Fort Worth. Even as he worked in a full-time ministry
position, he sometimes felt the same condemnation
that I had experienced as a teenager. There were
several members of the churches he served who were
legalistic, and they said some pretty negative things
about the pastors. For example, when Troy fell asleep
in the sun and got a terrible sunburn, a couple of
people suggested that he needed to address the sin in
his life because that was surely the reason why he got
sunburned.

Troy had an incredibly soft heart for kids whom
others had a hard time loving, and he invited them to
join the youth group. Sadly, the parents of some of the
other teens were concerned that the "bad" kids he was
drawing into the youth group were a bad influence on
the "good" kids. They told him to stop, and he said,

"What, stop bringing kids who need to know the love of Jesus to church?" Really?!

Like many pastors, he didn't share his concerns and hurts with others. Instead he tried to deal with them internally. Over time, his internal struggles and criticism from others wore him down, and he left the ministry. He just got fed up with it. He worked in a series of jobs but was never happy. God had called him to full-time ministry, and he was struggling to find a different place in the world.

Troy was still one of the most loving people you could imagine. You would never know he was in a bad place because he was always smiling. He never talked about himself; he always asked about you.

Then, when he didn't show up at work one day, his boss was worried and called Tracy. When Tracy called Troy and didn't get an answer, she became even more concerned. Tracy had two-year-old Austin with her, so she called her mom to drive with her to Troy's apartment.

Tracy felt in her spirit that something was wrong as they drove. Something bad had happened. Austin, sitting in his car seat in the back, must have heard her talking about it with her mom, because he took the sucker out of his mouth and said, "He's safe." Then he put his sucker back in.

Tracy wasn't prepared for anything else. Besides being her brother, Troy was one of her best friends growing up. They were such a close family and had never experienced the problems I grew up with.

She parked in front of Troy's apartment, and her mom went to the door. Tracy got out and stood beside the car, with Austin still inside. She heard her mom scream like she had never heard before. She felt it all the way to her core, and she ran into the apartment. Troy had taken his own life.

In such a short time, I had lost my mom, Tracy had lost her brother, and Sue and Steve had lost their son. It was a devastating time in our lives. Tracy reflects on her pain:

My world shut down. I had relied on God for so much, but never in a time like this. My parents had always been strong in their faith all my life, but none of us knew how to get through this or how God would help us. I had never questioned God before.

John's soccer team photo from high school.

John, his brother, Mike, and their church pastor.

John and Tracy during her senior year of high school.

John and Tracy on their wedding day.

John and his dad on his college graduation day.

John's brother, Mike, John, and his dad.

Tracy's family (Steve, Troy, and Sue) and John and Tracy.

John holding baby Austin in the hospital.

John and Tracy celebrating Austin's first birthday.

John and Austin snap a picture before
Austin's first day of preschool.

John, Tracy, and baby Ashtyn.

Austin and Ashtyn in elementary school.

John's family at their home in the summer of 2020.

It was hard to go to church because I didn't want to talk about what had happened. This was the place where Troy had come as a young man and had grown up spiritually—where he made his decision to go into ministry. The people asking about him were mostly well-meaning. Maybe in some ways I was a little embarrassed; things like that didn't happen in my family.

So many people said, "I know what you're going through," and I wanted to say, "No, you don't."

I went to a different level of learning how to trust God and know the character of God through His Word, but I was also at a place in my heart where I didn't want to go to church.

Then on a Sunday morning at Oak Cliff, the pastor, Tom Wilson, came to me and said, "I was praying last night for you, and I asked God to show me the pain in your heart."

At that moment Tom's eyes filled with tears as he said, "And he did. He showed me."

He didn't need to say anything else. For the first time I knew someone understood what I was feeling. Tom really knew and saw the excruciating pain I was feeling inside, and God was showing me a new side of Himself—how He loves. That revelation drove me to want to know God in a new way. I began to seek Him more. The Scripture came to life—truly the living Word of God comforted me.

—Tracy

TRACY'S NEW PASSION

Tracy began a long-term Bible study that Scott Wilson led at our church. Even though she had been strong in her faith all her life, she was not bold enough to speak up about it. The study, *Equipping the Saints*, was designed to train and prepare Christians to disciple other Christians. The study required a lot of Scripture memorization—hundreds of passages.

"Tracy is brilliant," Scott says, "but you would have never known it back then because she was so quiet and reserved. Then, as she spent time in the class working with others, she began to come out of her shell, speaking and sharing boldly."

Tracy says of that time, "Going through the loss of John's mom and my brother, and even the loss of our material possessions, we came to realize that those material possessions didn't matter to us anymore. *People* matter to us more than anything besides Christ, and God took me to new level of boldness to connect with other people."

A PASSION FOR PASTORS

Troy's death also opened our eyes and hearts to the trials pastors face and the criticism they hear when they don't do things "the way they've always been done." We weren't at Oak Cliff when Tom Wilson led it to become a multicultural congregation, but Scott said when his father began hiring Black and Hispanic staff members, several members of the church board were so upset with the change that they left. Still, Tom knew he was following God's instructions.

After Troy died, I began to see Jesus's final words to His disciples in a new light. Hours before He was arrested, Jesus was preparing the disciples for the transition that was coming with His death when He told them, "I am the vine; you are the branches. If you remain in me and I in you, you will bear much fruit; apart from me you can do nothing . . . As the

Father has loved me, so have I loved you. Now remain in my love" (John 15:5, 9).

He then spoke of the disciples' relationship with the world. "If the world hates you," He told them, "keep in mind that it hated me first" (John 15:18).

Wow! Jesus warned His disciples that the world would hate His disciples down through the ages.

God gives pastors the responsibility to teach, train, and send out disciples. He asks those of us in the congregation to lift up our pastors with prayers and encouragement. Instead, I think pastors often feel judged and condemned. The church places unrealistic expectations on them that we ourselves could not and generally do not live up to. The Lord has reminded me over the years that they are human and just trying to follow the call on their life like you and me. They put their pants on every morning just like us, and they have struggles, problems, and heartaches just like us.

Too many pastors carry the burdens of their position without feeling lifted up by the church members around them. They're not good about confiding in others with their own issues. They need our prayers, our love, and our friendship every day to stand strong and to know they are not leading and pastoring alone.

We must love others as Christ loves us and love our neighbors (and pastors) as ourselves.

7

GOD'S NEW
DIRECTION FOR US

I had been at the Annuity Board about two years when the Lord began stirring me to start doing something new. He spoke to me during my prayer time and said, "I want you to start a homebuilding business."

That seemed like a strange instruction. I was just getting started in a business career, and Tracy was still in college. I tried to make sense of starting something new at this point. But then the Lord gave me two reasons for becoming a homebuilder: reach people for Christ and give to the Kingdom.

"I want you to develop a business plan and budget and start praying over it," He told me. "And when you build your budget, I want you to have enough money to have date nights with Tracy. Don't make the budget so tight that you can't do anything, because that's not how I want to take care of My kids."

I told Tracy what I felt God was saying, and we prayed about it together that night. We both felt this was what the Lord was telling us to do.

Scott Wilson, the youth pastor who ticked me off the first time we met, had actually become one of my best friends by then (and still is to this day). He and I were playing golf about a month later, and after we teed off, I told him what we felt the Lord telling us. "I really feel like God's been telling me I'm supposed to be a homebuilder."

"Really?" Scott said a little sarcastically. "And how many homes have you built?"

"None."

"I don't understand," he said.

Scott's father-in-law was a homebuilder so he had some understanding of the business.

"I don't understand either," I said, "but the Lord told me that I'm supposed to be building homes."

We talked all the way down the fairway, and I explained what I had sensed God telling me in my prayer time. He wanted me to start a homebuilding business to reach people for Christ and give to the Kingdom. I didn't know what that would look like, but I was sure that was the message.

As we walked over to take our second shots, Scott said, "I think this may be the Lord. If you and Tracy feel like this is God, then let's dedicate it right now and ask Him to show you how to do it."

So we stopped right there in the middle of the fairway—there was nobody waiting on the tee—and Scott prayed, "God, we're sensing right now that this is what You're saying, and You're going to lead. You're going to open the door and make the provision. You're going to show us. We dedicate this moment to You, and we're going to do whatever You tell us to do."

Over the next few days, the steps became clear to me. Tracy and I developed a business plan and created a budget, and then we waited for the Lord to say, "Go." But God did not act quickly.

REVEALING MY PRIDE...AGAIN

My work at the Annuity Board was going well. Tracy graduated with her IT degree and got a good job with Cap Gemini, an international business and technology consulting company. We were both driving into Dallas every day to work, and Austin was staying with Tracy's mom. It was a good situation for us. We were paying our tithe and our bills, and we were finally repaying our student loans, which were not wiped out by bankruptcy. We had a little extra money for date nights and eating out occasionally. Our hard work was paying off, but I knew we had a long way to go financially. The Lord was helping us grow in our faith, but we still believed our success depended on ourselves working hard enough rather than God's provision.

One day, Austin—almost three at the time—stood with one hand on the coffee table in our living room, staring off into space in deep thought. I said, "Son, what are you thinking about?"

"I was thinking about King Nebuchadnezzar," he said, "and how God made him eat grass like an ox and have claws like an eagle."

I was like, "What?"

I'd graduated from Bible college, but I didn't have a clue what he was talking about. Austin had always loved the Word of God; he wanted us to read it to him every day. He also loved watching Bible stories on DVD, and he must have seen this one.

I said, "I don't remember that story, so let me look it up." I pulled my Bible out and I looked up the story. The first thing I saw was that Nebuchadnezzar had proudly looked out over His kingdom and thought, "Look at all I have done." Then God took it all away from him.

Immediately, I felt the Holy Spirit using that story to ask me, "Son, when are you going to learn?"

I had continued to believe that my childhood success, our house, and the other nice things in our lives were the result of our business sense, diligence, and hard work.

The Holy Spirit wanted me to spend time in prayer listening to what He was trying to tell me. I felt Him saying, "This is what I've been trying to teach you for all these years. I've allowed you to go through all these trials to show you that, even when you were a boy, I was the one taking care of you. You weren't smart enough to build the lawncare business or make money. You weren't the one taking care of yourself. I was the one taking care of you. And now, if you'll just give it all to Me, your whole heart, soul, mind, finances, dreams, and everything else and do it *My* way, not your way, then your whole life will change. You will have a full, abundant life."

I truly thought I had given it all to God, but I had not. As I was in the bedroom praying, I said, "God, first please forgive me for living my life for me, my way. Whatever You tell me from this day forward, I am going to do it. Everything I am and have is Yours. I give it to You. We're going to use everything we have in whatever way You tell us to use it."

We are not perfect at this, but we try to follow Christ's direction. Sometimes we miss it, but we try to get back on course and live to please Him. I think that pleases Him. And praise the Lord, He didn't make me eat grass!

WAITING FOR THE LORD

Though God's instructions to start a homebuilding company seemed clear, we waited for months for Him to give us the go-ahead to begin. All the while, I drove to Dallas every day to work at the Annuity Board. Fortunately, I had a great situation at work. Although I still didn't like IT, I asked God to help me each day to faithfully do that job with excellence. One of my bosses, Paul McGinnis, was also a mentor. Like everyone in our office, he cared about people. He also modeled strong leadership. God was using Tracy, Austin, Tracy's parents, Scott, and others to soften my heart at home and at church. Paul and others at the Annuity Board were showing me how to lead with compassion and strength at work.

Ashtyn, our little girl and my princess, was born in October 2001. I still believed God wanted us to start a new business, but we seemed to be moving further from that reality. Things were more complicated because of the recent September 11, 2001, attacks, which changed the whole world and had a direct impact on Tracy's work situation and our family.

Cap Gemini was a French company doing business all over the world. The Dallas office was multicultural and, after September 11, many of the foreign professionals working there did not feel comfortable traveling so much. As a result, Tracy picked up some of their relationships and had to travel a lot more to meet with clients across the country. She flew out every Sunday night and came home on Thursday night. It was so hard for her to leave the children and me every week.

Plus, this situation was making it harder, not easier, for us to start a homebuilding company. We needed Tracy's income (and then some) before I could leave my job. All that travel was not healthy for her or our family. As we continued to pray and seek God, we still felt strongly that somehow God was going to open the door to a new chapter in our lives. We just didn't have a clue how or when.

Sometimes God gives you a feeling—not particular words or Scripture, but just a feeling—that one season is ending and another is about to begin. Tracy had that feeling, and one Thursday night when she came home from a trip, she said she'd spent time praying and felt the Lord telling her to quit this job and look for another one. I was like, "WHAT?"

However, I trusted her, and she had always supported me in my job decisions, so we agreed to pray about it. Tracy and I have committed to each other that we will not discuss our personal feelings and opinions until *after* we pray. We don't want our personal opinions to skew the other person's ability to hear from the Lord. We have done this many times for many different reasons through the years.

She went to one room to pray while I went to another. We both wrote down what we felt like the Lord said and then came back together. We agreed that, if we didn't both hear the same thing, we would continue to pray until we both came together and had heard the same thing from the Lord. Well, that is what happened; we agreed and decided it was time to look.

She didn't send out a bunch of résumés—just one to the J.C. Penney corporate headquarters in Dallas.

We prayed before she sent it and asked God to do His will. As Tracy filled out the application, she paused at the "Desired Salary" line. She felt the Lord wanted her to write the exact amount we had been praying over in our budget—the budget we needed to start our business. A few days later, Penney's called and invited Tracy for an interview. After a couple of interviews, she was traveling on business to New York when a woman in human resources called and offered her the job. The job was in Dallas, and they offered a significant increase over her current salary.

Tracy called me and I was excited for her and us. "Are you going to take it?" I asked.

"No," she said. "The salary is $15,000 less than we said we need. I have to tell them no."

Tracy was trusting God more than ever at this point. God had told us He would provide the income we needed, and Tracy believed Him. She called Penney's and apologized, then said she couldn't take the job at the salary they were offering. She hoped they might reconsider, but we trusted God either way.

The woman in HR said the company would not be able to do that, and since the director who was hiring for the position was leaving the country for two weeks, we shouldn't expect to hear anything else for a while, if at all.

Tracy was alone working in New York City, disappointed that she would have to keep traveling and knowing she was turning down a good job for more money in Dallas. But she fully believed this was what the Lord wanted her to do.

An hour or so later, her phone rang. It was the HR representative from Penney's. "I don't understand how this happened or why," the woman said, "but they've agreed to pay you that salary. Plus, we'll include your five years at Cap Gemini as if you've been working at Penney's to calculate the amount of vacation time and profit sharing you are eligible to receive." Tracy hadn't even asked for that!

She called me with the news, and we both were overcome with gratitude to God. Tracy was coming home. And we were more financially secure than ever.

A month later, Tracy had started her new job, and I was driving to work—sitting in the same I-35 traffic I'd sat through for the past seven and a half years—and praying. I always prayed on my way to work. I was praying God would help me work hard and represent Him well. My heart had begun to shift a few years earlier because I knew the Lord was leading me to do something else, but I still wanted to represent Him well where He had me.

That morning as I was sitting in traffic right by the Dallas Zoo, I looked over at the huge giraffe sculpture out front and felt the Lord say, "Today's the day."

I said, "Today's the day for what?"

He said, "Today's the day to start the homebuilding business."

I said, "Whatchu talkin' about?" like the character from an old favorite TV show, *Diff'rent Strokes.*

God made clear what He was talking about. After five years of praying and waiting, it was finally time.

I hesitated just for a second, and in that moment of hesitation I heard the Lord say, "It's time to get out of the boat and walk on water. Are you going to get out of the boat and experience the miraculous? Or are you going to sit in the boat and watch other people experience the miraculous?"

"Yes," I said, "I'm getting out."

He said, "You can trust me."

I called Tracy as soon as I got to the office—we didn't have cell phones then—and told her.

"Okay," she said, "let's do it!"

Then I hung up the phone and thought about what a great place to work the Annuity Board had been for more than seven years. Great people and great benefits. I was off every other Friday. I had six weeks' vacation and a generous retirement account, not to mention I felt it was a secure income.

I got home that night, and Tracy said, "How did it go?"

"I couldn't do it," I said.

I had let the comfort of this world outweigh the step God was asking me to take. He had been faithful and fulfilled so many promises, but, for a day, my trust in Him wavered. Tracy and I prayed that night that God would help me. The next day I went to work and gave them my notice.

WISDOM AND MONEY

You can't build a house without money, and we didn't have any. A homebuilder also needs to know more than just how to saw a board and hammer a nail. I had done some framing and plumbing, so I knew my way around a job site—but I needed to learn more. Before I went to the bank, I called on three homebuilders to ask their advice. Two of them were successful, and one had gone out of business.

All three of them talked about the finances first. "Don't rob Peter to pay Paul," they said. "You have to stay on top of cash flow because if you start missing payments to subcontractors, word gets out fast. Don't overextend. Don't grow faster than you're able to."

The man who had been successful for the longest was more concerned about relationships than money, though. "Never get to the point where you don't like people," he said. "Buyers will naturally gripe and complain. They want everything to be perfect. You're going to make mistakes. But if you're not careful, you'll forget why you're in business and get to the point that you don't like people. If you ever get to that place, you need to get out of the business."

That stuck with me so much that now, years later, I still constantly remind our staff that, if we ever get to the place where we don't like people, we've missed the whole point. Especially as a believer, my philosophy is that God uses us to reach people and show them how much He loves them. I should value people because God does. Today we have six companies, but we know we are not in the homebuilding or the mortgage business. We are in the *people* business, and God just uses these other businesses to reach them. All the companies God has given us to steward are just vehicles for reaching people for Christ through relationships and giving profits to the kingdom.

THE BANKER LAUGHED AT ME

Before I could build that kind of business, though, I had to build my first house. That meant getting a bank loan. I explained to the banker that we wanted to build houses so we could reach people for Christ and give to the kingdom. I went on to explain that Tracy was a few months into a new job, we had two young children, I had never built a house before, and I didn't have a customer for the first house I planned to build.

The loan officer laughed at me. He sat behind his desk and literally laughed at me for asking the bank to lend me $120,000 to build a spec house. It reminded me of all those years ago when the banker laughed at us when we went to get a loan to build our first home. Sometimes the enemy attacks us in the middle of the miracle God is doing as we step out in faith. The enemy tried to get my temper and pride to rise and respond to their laughing, but God reminded me He was my source and I could trust Him.

The next day, I went to another bank. The loan officer there didn't laugh, but he did ask a valid question, "Why would we lend you any money?" I walked out feeling like the Israelites after they left Egypt only to find themselves out in the desert. Had God brought me here to fail?

That night Tracy and I spent a long time praying. I said, "God, we're trying to be faithful and obedient, but You're going to have to show up. We can't do this without You."

The next morning, I had an appointment with another bank vice president named Pam. I waited in her office and when she walked in—and you sort of have to be from Texas to understand this—she was a cowgirl. A red-haired cowgirl. I thought, *Oh, stink. This woman's going to be tough.*

We talked for a few minutes, and I explained that we wanted a loan to build spec houses so we could reach people for Christ and give to the kingdom.

"Oh, we don't do loans for spec houses," she said.

As she was talking, I felt the Holy Spirit saying, "Ask her what a spec house is."

Well, I couldn't do that. She was a banker. She obviously knew what a spec house was. But I asked her anyway.

"A spec house is one that you are building but you haven't sold," she said.

Then I felt the Holy Spirit prompt me to say, "Hypothetically, if you did spec loans, would you require me to personally guarantee it?"

I asked her, and she said, "Well, of course we would."

"Technically, then," I said, "it *would* be a sold job, because you'd have a guaranteed buyer: me."

"You know," she said, "I've never thought of it that way."

I was thinking, *Me neither!* but I didn't say it out loud.

We kept talking until she said, "You know what? We're going to do this loan." Yes!

We were in business. Sort of.

The bank required us to put $40,000 down, and draining my entire Annuity Board retirement account only got us halfway there. We needed another $20,000. Another huge roadblock.

By that time, Tracy and I had joined a small group at church. During our group prayer time the following week, I asked them to pray for a solution for us. One of the guys, an ophthalmologist, said, "Why don't I just lend you the money?"

"Really?" I said.

"Sure," he said. "Just pay me back when you can."

God had answered the prayer right then and there. With that, we were ready to start.

THE CLEANUP MAN

As we started construction on the first house, I felt God telling me, "I want you to do all the cleanup on every house for the first year, from cleaning the job site to cleaning the bathrooms—the whole house. I want you to experience every part of the process, because I want you to value every person involved in the process equally."

I had done manual labor since I was a kid, so I wasn't scared of hard work. However, nothing could have prepared me for cleaning urine out of a bathtub because some construction guys didn't think twice about peeing in someone else's tub. Any personal pride I felt about being "the boss" was gone. God taught me through that experience that the cleanup person is just as important as the CEO. It takes every one of us.

WRITING OUR PURPOSE
ON OUR HEARTS

Thank God, we had a buyer a few weeks before finishing work on the house. With a sales contract in hand, I went to the bank and asked if they would lend us money to start a second house. I explained to Pam that we would be giving some of the profits from the first house back to God. I'm sure she didn't think that was a wise business decision, but she agreed to lend us money to keep going.

In my prayer time the morning before closing on the first house, the Lord said, "Hey, I want to ask you something."

I said, "Okay, what is it?"

He said, "I'm going to ask you to give Me *all* the profit from this house. I'm not telling you that you have to, but I'm asking if you will trust Me with it. I want this business to be built on Me."

I talked with Tracy about it, and we agreed to do it.

After we closed and made our final payments to all the subcontractors and suppliers, we repaid the loans to the bank and my friend at church, and then we gave the rest of the money to the church.

A few months later, just before closing with the buyers of our second house, a similar thing happened. I was in my prayer time the morning of the closing, and I felt God saying, "I don't want these people to buy that house."

"Well, first of all, that's a big problem," I said, "because we have a contract and they're supposed to close today. That's a legal document. I can't just break it."

God said, "Trust me. I care about these people more than this house."

I had a sense after my prayer time that their marriage might be failing and only the wife was going to live in the house.

Less than fifteen minutes after I finished my prayers, my cell phone rang. It was the man, and he asked if I had a few minutes to talk.

"Sure," I said. "In fact, I need to talk to you."

"This might sound weird to you," I said, "but I'm just going to be honest with you. When I was praying this morning, I really felt like the Lord told me you guys are buying this house because you were getting a divorce and your wife is going to live in it without you."

He was quiet for a few seconds, and then I heard him crying. It was true.

I said, "The first thing the Lord wants you to know is that He loves you and your family very much. He loves you far more than this house. The Lord told me to let you out of the contract because He wants your family to stay together."

"Thank you," he said. He was quiet again, and then said, "Yes, you're right."

We cancelled the contract and sold the house to another family a few weeks later.

Ten years later, Tracy and I saw the couple and their children at a restaurant. They were still together.

When we started the company, our purpose was to reach people for Christ and give to the Kingdom. God used those first two homes to reinforce that purpose— to write it on our hearts in a way that it could never be erased. I never realized the Lord had actually done that until I began to write this book. As we follow Him, He continues to show us things He has been doing all along. Many times, I never recognized it while I was going through it, but sometime later I realized how God was at work.

We've had bankers, financial advisors, and accountants through the years disagree with our giving philosophy, but we've made a commitment to God. Whatever He tells us to do, that's what we're going to do, because Tracy and I firmly believe we don't own anything. Everything we have is His (Psalm 24:1).

8

COMING HOME TO A HEART OF LOVE

*A*s a brand-new homebuilder, I didn't have my choice of the best building lots. No subdivision developers were inviting us into their projects, so I spent a lot of my time driving around looking for lots. After we had built and sold about twenty homes, though, the developer of a community called Harmony in Red Oak invited us to buy lots and build homes in his subdivision. We hired Rob Poole, a friend from church with a gift for connecting with people, as our sales manager. He worked out of the construction trailer until we finished our first model home.

Rob's first challenge was to get people to visit our model home. We were building alongside some of the biggest homebuilders in the area, and their homes were a lot larger than ours. Our model was 1,800 square feet; theirs were 3,000 to 4,000 square feet. In 2005, size mattered. Building smaller homes gave us a lower price point, which we thought would attract buyers. Smaller homes also allowed us to use higher-quality materials and appliances than our larger competitors and still keep our costs down. But most of the people looking at homes in Harmony were attracted to the larger floor plans.

"We relied on our faith and on God to bring the customers we needed to sustain the company," Rob recalls. "We prayed every day for Him to bring people who might be interested. Several times, people told me, 'I don't know why, but I was driving by and felt like I needed to come in and meet with you guys.' We were able to sell six homes in 2005, which was enough to keep us in business."

Those six families became Rob's friends. He had met with them a couple of times a week while we were building their homes, and then he was at every closing. Closing on a home can be a stressful time, especially for buyers, and Rob's calm, reassuring demeanor made the process less stressful.

After the families moved in, they knew they could drop by the model home and see Rob if they ever had questions about the house.

"Sometimes, they still stop by just to visit or ask me to pray for things that they're experiencing in their lives," Rob says. "The relationship just continues, and then they bring people who might be looking for a new home. It all becomes part of their experience with our company."

He continues, "Keeping people's trust throughout the relationship is so important to us. I've heard so many stories of builders not doing what they said they would. And we have difficulties sometimes. But John has created a company where it's not about winning or getting your way; it's about doing the right thing. That builds relationships. And it lets us sleep at night."

CREATING AN EFFICIENT, CARING ORGANIZATION

While Rob was focused on maintaining a good relationship with our customers, Tracy and I did our best to maintain good relationships with our growing team members. I was thankful for a lesson I learned years earlier when I was at the Annuity Board. My boss assigned a project to me to conduct a time/motion study of people in the office. This wasn't a manufacturing plant or a distribution facility where people were constantly in motion; this was an office filled with white-collar workers who sat at their desks most of the day. My project was to observe them and use a stopwatch to time everything they did. I took notes on each task—when they started, when they stopped, and everything they did in between, including their phone calls.

After several weeks of collecting the data, we determined that we were overstaffed by about twenty-four people. I'm sure that, if they had done similar studies throughout the entire organization, they would have found we were overstaffed in every department. The leadership team faced a difficult decision: either let some people go or operate at a financial disadvantage in a field that was growing more competitive.

They chose not to let anybody go.

I appreciated the compassion they demonstrated for their employees, but by putting the company at a competitive disadvantage, they risked the possibility of even more layoffs down the road.

The lesson for me was that a lean, efficient organization can also be the most compassionate. Hiring too many people exposes them to the chance of being let go later, but a company can't be understaffed either. It takes wisdom to strike the right balance. I am reminded frequently that this is the Lord's businesses, and He has given me the responsibility to steward it well. We are in the people business first, but we must remember He called us to reach people for Christ and give to the kingdom. I can reach people for Christ, but I will be out of business if I don't make a profit. On the other hand, making and giving money to the kingdom without loving people shows that I am really just in it for the money. We must stay focused on both.

As our companies continue to grow, Tracy and I must divide our limited one-on-one time among more people, giving us less time to spend with each one. That's been one of the most difficult parts of building these businesses. I enjoy every relationship and feel so blessed the Lord allows me to live life with each one and that they allow me to be part of their lives.

TEN-CENT TOUCHPOINTS

Paul McGinnis, my mentor at the Annuity Board, had hundreds of people reporting to him, because others had recognized that he was brilliant, and he loved people. As a reminder to connect with people all day long, he suggested that I put ten dimes in my left pocket every morning, and each time I connected with somebody—not just a quick conversation, but a real connection—I should move one of those dimes to my right pocket. The goal every day, of course, was to move all the dimes into my right pocket.

I don't carry ten dimes anymore but I still live by the principle. That's how I learn how the company and our people are doing. That's where we build relationships. If I'm driving around subdivisions where we're building homes, I get out of the truck and try to listen more than I talk to the employees we have on site.

We have expanded on this principle by identifying sixty "touchpoints"—opportunities to interact and connect with the lives of people with every home we build. Each of those touchpoints is an opportunity to share the love of Christ.

For every home we build, we come in contact with at least ten potential buyers. Forty-two people build the home, and eight more assist in the closing. So if we close six hundred and fifty homes this year, that comes to thirty-nine thousand touchpoints, and each one matters. They give my team and me the opportunity to share the hope that is in us. At the end of the process, we hope many of those touchpoints develop into lifelong relationships.

A PLACE TO BUILD OUR NEW HOME

I answered the phone one morning a few years ago, and the lady on the other end said, "Is this John Houston?"

"Yes, ma'am," I said.

"My name is Mrs. Ranton," she said, "and I hope it's okay if I call you."

"Yes, ma'am."

"Because I was praying the other day, and I felt like God was telling me you were supposed to buy my property."

"Oh, really?" I said. The Holy Spirit jabbed my heart right then and reminded me not to be sarcastic with this nice woman.

"Yes," she said.

I was skeptical. Through the years several people had told me the same thing about their property and then wanted far more than it was worth.

Mrs. Ranton seemed sweet, and I knew she believed what she was telling me about her property west of Waxahachie.

"Thank you for calling," I said. "Send me some information, and I'll have someone from our company take a look at it."

She had something different in mind. God was telling her that her property was for *my* family to live on.

Her timing could not have been worse. Tracy and I wanted to build a home out in the country, and after ten years of praying and looking, we had found a pretty, two-hundred-acre tract about five miles from Mrs. Ranton's land. We had already bought the property and had it laid out. The plan was to develop all but about ten acres for ourselves, and we were working to get everything permitted.

"Why don't you just pray about it," she said, "and let me know if you're interested."

"Yes, ma'am," I said.

About thirty days went by, and I hadn't prayed about that property at all. It wasn't out of rebellion; I honestly hadn't given it a second thought. But Mrs. Ranton had. She called back and said, "Mr. Houston, this is Mrs. Ranton. I just wanted to see if you had thought any more about my property."

"Well, no, not really," I said. "I've got to be honest with you ...."

She cut me off. "I know you think I'm just a little old lady, but I want you to understand, I really do believe God's telling me this. And I don't want you to think that I tell people this very often. This property is very special to me. Our family has owned it since the 1800s. I was born out there, and my parents were born out there."

Then she chuckled and said, "So will you do an old widow a favor and meet me out there?"

Well, how are you going to say no to that? I said, "Yes ma'am, I will."

I met her out there, and we stood at the front of the property. She said again, "I prayed about this, and I really just feel like the Lord is saying this is a property that you and your family could live on."

I thanked her again, but I didn't explain how complicated it would be to change our plans. Two other families were involved, and we had all felt God leading us to the property south of Midlothian.

Two weeks later, Melanie Brewer, our land and lot acquisitions manager, and I were driving some subdivisions in Waco, and I was thinking about Mrs. Ranton's property. In fact, I'd been thinking about it a lot—so much that I wondered if God might be speaking to Mrs. Ranton after all. On the way back to the office, I told Melanie we should swing by and take another look. Melanie and her husband had been our friends for twenty years. They and other dear friends were also looking for a place to build, and we all wanted to be close to one another.

We got out of the truck, and I felt something…like this was the place for us. "I really believe this might be where the Lord is leading us," I said.

Over the next few days, all three couples asked God to give us guidance. He clearly spoke to each of us quickly and said, "Yes, I want this to be your sanctuary. I'm going to give you a place of peace here, a place of rest for you and a place where people will come and feel my presence. They'll feel the peace of the Lord." Needless to say, we bought the property, built our homes there, and used the other large piece of land we had bought to build homes for buyers.

DISCOVERING A FATHER'S LOVE

When the Lord told us it was time to start a family, I didn't understand how that was going to work financially. I was still in college, Tracy had taken a break from college to get a better job, and I was working thirty hours a week between classes and studying to pay the bills. But we believed that was what He was telling us to do.

We didn't discuss this with anybody. Then a few weeks later in church, a man walked over to Tracy and said, "God has given you the gift you want. And he is going to be a great teacher of the Word."

Tracy knew exactly what the man was talking about. We believe in the gift of prophecy, and this man was giving Tracy a word from the Lord. Not long after that, her doctor confirmed that she was pregnant, and Austin was born on January 2, 1998.

When Austin was a little boy, he wanted us to read Scripture to him—not just tell him Bible stories but read straight from the Bible. His desire felt to us as if God was preparing him to be a great teacher of the Word, but we didn't know exactly what that may look like for him.

I was a stern father as Austin and Ashtyn grew up. Because I had grown up without my parents at home from age eleven, I had to learn to take care of myself when I was very young. There were pros and cons to that, and it's been one of the bigger struggles in our marriage, our family, and in business.

I expected my children to take on more responsibility than they were ready for. I was way over the
top pushing, challenging, and leading by rules and not
love. I didn't know what it looked like for kids to be
kids. Tracy had to tell me (many times), "No, the kids
don't need to learn to mow the lawn when they're six
years old."

My relationship with our children when they were
younger reminds me now of the Christian legalism
I sometimes experienced and grew to believe in,
because I didn't understand God's unconditional love.
I knew better by the time I became a father. God had
shown me His grace and forgiveness a thousand times
over. He had taught me to love the book of Romans in
the Bible, which teaches us we are no longer under the
law. The law is still in place for us to recognize our sin,
but it is God's love that draws us in.

Yet I was still hard on Austin, leading by the law
instead of by love. Thankfully, God showed patience
with me. He gave me time to correct myself. By Austin's
early teens, though, it was time for God to give me a
wake-up call.

At about age fifteen, Austin started acting out in
some seriously rebellious ways, and I pushed him

even harder to straighten up. At the same time, I was beyond stressed with a full plate at work. I'm afraid to say I brought the stress home and let it affect my marriage. Tracy and I were sort of nipping at each other a lot more than usual. All this left me spiritually frustrated, unable to focus where I should have. I thought I had done so much for God; why wasn't He taking care of these issues for me? Why was I having to deal with problems with my son, my work, and my marriage?

Then one day out of the blue, a local pastor came to my friend and pastor, Scott Wilson, and said, "I think God gave me a word for John Houston. You know him, don't you?"

Scott said he did and offered to set up a breakfast for the three of us. I wasn't thrilled with the idea, but I went along. We were sitting at the table having some polite conversation when the pastor stiffened a bit and asked if he could share something with me. He started with, "I'm just the messenger. I'm just telling you what I believe God has told me to share with you."

Then he said, "I believe the Lord is giving you a word out of Romans, chapter two: 'You didn't think, did you, that just by pointing your finger at others you would distract God from seeing all your misdoings and from coming down on you hard? Or did you think that because he's such a nice God, he'd let you off the hook? Better think this one through from the beginning. God is kind, but he's not soft. In kindness he takes us firmly by the hand and leads us into a radical life-change' " (Romans 2:3–4, The Message).

That sort of ticked me off, but he was just getting warmed up. Next he said, "The Lord is saying that, if you don't change the way you're living, you're going to lose your son."

Well, this guy didn't even know *me*, let alone Austin, and that was the stupidest thing I had ever heard. My relationship with God and my son was none of his business. I was polite for the rest of our breakfast, but I was so upset when I got to my truck that I decided not to go to work. I went home to pray and figure out what was going on.

I read the Bible, prayed, and journaled all day, but God didn't give me an answer. The next morning in my prayer time, I continued working through these thoughts, praying for an answer. Nothing. I had to go to work and put it aside until the next morning.

Finally, after three days, the Lord spoke to me through the same verse the pastor had spoken. "I'm a kind God, which means I love you, but I'm not a soft God. Just because this is the way you've always been living doesn't mean it's okay. And I'm not going to let you keep getting away with it. But because I'm a kind God and I love you, I'm going to lead you to radical life change. I'm going to be the one that takes you there."

Then He gave me a vision: Austin was about five years old and he wanted to run off, but I held his hand so he couldn't because he was so small.

God said to me, "You need to understand that you are a condemning, manipulating father and husband. You are leading by law, not by love, because you don't know *how* to love. You have never understood my love. And because you don't understand the love of your heavenly Father, you don't know how to love your kids, and you don't know how to love your wife."

What a crushing message to hear from God. Tracy and I had been married for twenty years, and I had tried to follow the loving model her parents had given. I had busted my butt to grow and change in the way God wanted me to. I had tried my best to do everything He asked me to do. Now God was telling me I had failed and that the pastor was right. I was losing my son.

God said, "I'm going to teach you, but there are some things in your life that you're going to have to change."

Honestly, this really ticked me off. For years, everything I had been doing was for Him, from the time I woke up until the time I went to bed. I had started every morning with an hour or longer in prayer and reading Scripture. We had built our company with the purpose of reaching people for Christ and giving to the kingdom. I was doing the very best I knew to do for God!

I heard Him say, "That's all great, but if you do all those things without love, everything is meaningless."

Everything. Was. Meaningless.

So . . . now what?

Over the next year and a half, God continually reminded me to love people where they were. He showed me specific things I had done for which I needed to ask forgiveness from Tracy, Austin, and Ashtyn, and I did. I went to her parents, my dad, and probably another thirty people all the way back to a girl I dated in high school and asked for their forgiveness for particular things the Lord showed me I had done that did not represent Him. Through those actions, God was softening my heart.

Then He said He would reveal to me where Austin was, but I would have to trust Him. I didn't realize how frightening that would be. After months and months, I tried to talk with Austin about where I thought God wanted us to be. This was the boy who had grown up loving to read and hear God's Word. Things were different now, he told me. "The bottom line," he said, "is that I don't think I even believe in the same God you do. I think we're headed into different directions. And we're just going to have to learn to deal with that."

How could I "learn to deal with that"? My son didn't believe in God?

One morning, I journaled the words I thought God was speaking: "I want you to take Austin to any concert he wants to go to, anywhere in the United States, and I want you to be okay with it."

As I read back over those words, I knew they couldn't be from God. It didn't make sense. One of our biggest arguments was over the music Austin was listening to. I believe music dramatically impacts your heart and thinking, because whatever you're putting in your brain is what comes out through your beliefs, words, and actions.

I talked to Tracy and Scott and we all prayed about it. In time, I came to realize God really did want me to take Austin to a concert. I wanted to be obedient, so I sat down with Austin and Tracy and told him I would take him to any concert he chose.

The next day, Austin said he wanted to go to the Beach Goth festival in Orange County, California. I couldn't imagine anything worse. In my mind, Beach Goth was some of the darkest of the dark music (even though I didn't really understand what it was). And yet, God was telling me to do this.

I said okay.

For the next several days, I prayed, "Why, God? Why in the world are You telling me to take my own child into this awful place? This makes no sense."

God reminded me that I had spent a lot of time with Austin over the years, but I really didn't *know* my son. I hadn't taken the time to understand him. God was telling me to get to know him as a person. That was one of the goals of this trip, so we went a few days early just to hang out and do whatever he wanted.

The night before the concert, in the middle of the night, the Lord woke me up and said, "Son, this is the reason you're here: you're meeting Austin at the well. You have to understand that's where he's at."

I felt God reminding me of the Bible's account in John chapter four of a Samaritan woman that Jesus met at the community well. He asked her to bring Him some water, and she reminded Him that a Samaritan woman shouldn't be serving a Jew for cultural reasons. She was a woman seeking truth, and Jesus revealed to her that He knew who she was, the life she was living, and He understood her deepest need—to find "living water." God was telling me that Austin was searching, and unless I knew and understood my son, I could not help him.

Then He told me, "But I don't want you to tell Austin why you're here. I just want you to love him where he's at. If the day comes that he asks you why you brought him here, then you can tell him then. I don't want you to tell him until he asks because this is about Me, not about you. I had you bring Austin here because the day will come when he asks, 'Why did I take my dad to a concert like this?' And when you tell him, I will reveal to him that everywhere he goes, he is taking Me. I am always with him."

He continued, "So when you go to the concert, just follow him around. Go wherever he wants to go. It's going to be wild and crazy to you. Just pray in the Spirit behind him. Just be with him."

We finally arrived at the concert the next morning, and the crowd was like nothing I had ever seen. Droves of people dressed all in black like a dark cloud filled the whole place. We decided to leave for a little while, but when we came back later, the guy at the gate said we couldn't get back in. Our tickets didn't allow reentry once we left. But then he said, "Hey, but you two look cool. Father and son."

I wonder how many of those he saw? Fortunately, he let us back in. We stayed for another couple of hours, then Austin was ready to go.

About six months later, Tracy and I were in the kitchen one night when Austin came in. "Dad," he said, "I have a question. I still have friends asking me why in the world you would take me to a concert like that. I don't know the answer. So . . . why *did* you?"

I was able to share the whole story with him, just as God promised.

I still believe the prophecy Tracy heard before Austin was born, that our son would be a great teacher of the Word. I also know that God is the greatest teacher, and I pray every day that He will keep teaching me. I want to have a heart that listens to God and then acts on it so my mind is continually transformed and renewed (Romans 12:2).

I am humbled as I look back on those days with Austin. They may have been some of the hardest times of my life. The son I loved dearly didn't love me and didn't really want to have anything to do with me—because I *told* him I loved him with my words, but I didn't *show* him with my actions.

Thanks to the grace of God, I have a healthy and loving relationship with Austin today. He is about to graduate from university and works full-time with Tracy and me in one of our companies. We are both continuing to grow closer to Christ as we learn more about His unconditional love and the truth in His Word. I am so blessed and honored to be Austin's dad and friend. Oh, and by the way—he owns the house next door to us, and we are so happy to have him as our next-door neighbor.

As I continue to learn that I am a sinner who falls short of the glory of God and that God forgives me, I am faster to love and forgive others. We are all learning and growing—my wife, my kids, my friends, employees, my pastor ... and definitely me.

COMING HOME

My father's brother Sam would have been the first to tell you he hadn't lived an exemplary life. He was an alcoholic for years, and his drinking almost killed him. In the hospital on oxygen, his doctors said they were sending him home, and he would be dead within two months.

Maybe for the first time, my uncle considered his life, and he didn't like what he saw. You might call it a deathbed confession, but the first time Uncle Sam called out to Jesus, He heard his cry and changed his life.

I was in my twenties at the time, and even though I didn't see him often, his dramatic change had an impact on me. He was sold out for Jesus, and two months after he left the hospital, even though he had not stopped drinking, there was a difference in him. In fact, my uncle lived for several more years.

One weekend, he called my dad and said he was planning a barbecue at his house in two weeks. He wanted the whole family and all his friends to come. "This will be the last time you see me," he said. He believed he was dying, but this time he was ready. Of course, everybody went.

Tracy and I were married then, and we drove out to my uncle's house. While we were there, he asked everybody for two minutes alone with him. Tracy and I sat down with him, and he told us, "First, I want to apologize for the way I lived my life. I wasn't a good model, but I have accepted Jesus as my Savior, and I want you to have an opportunity to know Him." We assured him that we were confident in our relationship with Christ.

Just days later, Dad called and told me his brother had died.

I rode to the funeral with my dad—two and half hours in the car talking, just the two of us. It was the first deep conversation I ever remember having with him, and it became a turning point in our relationship.

We talked about his mom, his brother, my mom, and my growing-up years.

Dad talked about his own difficult childhood. Like me, he didn't grow up in his parents' house. His mom loved him dearly but was unable be the mother he needed, so his grandmother took care of him.

I knew there had been times when I looked at my father with anger and hard feelings, but that begin to change in me after our long drive. I tried not to blame him for his mistakes. After all, parents raise their children to the best of their abilities. I never knew how hard a job that is until I became a parent myself. Driving down the long Texas interstate that day, we each admitted mistakes, and we forgave each other.

Dad and I started spending more time together from that point on. He had fully devoted his life to Christ and was growing in his relationship with Him. He was involved in a divorce care group at his church, and he met the woman who would become his wife, Debbie.

Dad moved to Midlothian and was highly involved in the community. He was elected to the Midlothian City Council and ultimately elected mayor in 2012. He started a prayer group that met every week in his office. With Debbie's influence—she loved being with family—Dad began spending more time with our children and coming to their events at school. They called regularly to make sure they didn't miss anything important in Austin's and Ashtyn's lives.

Across the road from us, on part of Mrs. Ranton's property where God promised a place of peace, Dad and Debbie built their home. Tracy's parents have a home next door to them.

Around the corner, our pastor and his wife, Scott and Jenni Wilson, built their home. Yes, the same man I was so irritated with over twenty-five years ago for telling me to "just go pray and ask the Lord what He wants [me] to do, what He wants [me] to say, where He wants [me] to go." Yep, Scott Wilson, the one who called me out and said, "Don't take the easy way out by me telling you what I think," but instead said to go spend time with God and ask Him what He wants. Scott is one of my very best friends in this world.

I am blessed and thankful to still have a relationship with my brother and sister today. Mike is still married to Carrie, and they live with their beautiful family just about ten miles away. He runs his own business, and John Houston Custom Homes partners with him frequently. Cora lives in a town just outside of Waco and is married with a beautiful family of her own. I am so thankful for both of them. God continues to show me, through them, through our children, and through so many more people how to build a home.

My children helped me learn this: the Word of God is God. His Word is His heart, and the best way to know His heart is to read, study, and meditate on His Word as if it is God talking directly to me. As I read it, He is speaking. As I meditate on it throughout the day, I am entering His heart again, and asking Him to use His Spirit and His Word to transform me. This is how He shows me *His* love and how He shows me *how* to love.

In my childhood, my parents created an imperfect home that left my brother, my sister, and me vulnerable to the dangers of the world. As a father, I created an imperfect home where I pushed away my own son.

Now I know that God's heart is my true home. Every morning when I kneel before Him and listen to Him speak to me through His Word, I am entering into His heart, my home. There, I experience His peace and joy, His hope and love. I can stay there all day—not literally in the prayer closet but in His heart.

Jesus said, "In my Father's house are many mansions: if it were not so, I would have told you. I go to prepare a place for you" (John 14:2 KJV).

Said another way, there's plenty of room in His heart for all of us to find our way home.

EPILOGUE

A week before I started working on this book, I got a text from one of my favorite young leaders in our homebuilding company that asked, "Can I meet with you today?"

Justin had been working with us for eight years, and I couldn't remember him ever asking to meet me on such short notice. I knew it must have been important.

"Sure," I replied. I suggested a fast-food restaurant nearby.

Justin was thirty years old, and I could picture him running the company one day. He's that good, both in his character and his capability. He had worked summers with us when he was in college, weed-eating ditches, pressure-washing garages, and other manual labor jobs. We were building about forty homes a year then, so I knew everybody in the company. It didn't take long for me to realize I wanted Justin to come to work for us when he graduated from Texas A&M.

In 2011, we had an opening. He came to the house, and we prayed together. We both felt God saying this was the right opportunity, and I hired Justin as an estimator, a job I had done in the past. He learned the business fast, moving up to superintendent and then area construction manager, overseeing construction of hundreds of homes.

Driving to meet with him after his text, something in my spirit told me Justin was thinking of leaving the company. Immediately I was frustrated with myself for not letting him know how important he was to us— for allowing another company to make him an offer that he would consider. Justin had two young children with a third on the way, so he had to consider how best to take care of his family.

I was really hoping he would stay. God had helped Tracy and me grow our business into a family of six companies. A key to that growth has been talented leaders like Justin who remind me of the lessons God has taught me and enable me to be the leader God wants me to be. By the time I arrived at the restaurant to meet him, I had many different ideas on how to keep him and even created in my head a new position for him reporting directly to me, in preparation for greater leadership opportunities. I was already looking forward to working more closely with him. I was excited for his future but also ready to hear what was going on in his heart.

When we sat at the table, I could tell he was uncomfortable. I wanted to say, "Relax, Justin. It's going to be all right." But I had to wait to hear what he had to say.

"This is one of the hardest things I've ever done," he said. "But I have to give you my resignation."

"Why are you doing that?"

He said, "About sixty days ago, God started speaking to me, telling me it was time for me to get out of the boat. He said He wants to show me the miraculous."

For a moment I couldn't speak. Justin was telling my own story back to me.

"Then, last night at nine o'clock," he said, "I felt His voice speaking to me and saying, 'Son, I've been stirring your heart, and I've been asking you to step out of the boat and trust Me, and now it's time.' "

There are times in your life when you feel the presence of the Holy Spirit—the warmth, the power, the tingling. The Spirit was there at the table with Justin and me. I had to hold on to keep the tears from welling up.

I set my thoughts and ideas aside. I couldn't try to convince Justin to stay. Because if I'm teaching and training leaders while holding onto them for myself, then I'm just doing it for me. Nothing could be more selfish.

I was suddenly thrilled for Justin and for the exciting things God was about to show him because he was choosing to trust Jesus. I encouraged him to follow God's voice, and I said, "I'd like to help you, if I can. I'll provide seed money or lend you whatever you need to get your business started."

"I can't do that," he said.

"Why not?"

He was quiet for a moment, then he said, "Because God told me I can trust Him with this. Just Him. So that's what I have to do."

Wow!

Then he said that about a year earlier, God had given him a vision. "In that vision, I saw that I was one day going to stand before God see a reflection of myself. And in that reflection, I would see if I had become the man that God called me to be."

So Justin stepped out of the boat. He's trusting God.

We hear God's voice, we follow God's voice, and we step out in faith believing God's voice.

Then He will lead us home. Oh, what an adventure the journey will be!

ACKNOWLEDGEMENTS

When I sensed God wanted me to share my story, I knew I would need help to take all that was in my heart and mind and put it into words that would bless and encourage others. This book is the result of so many people who have believed in me and demonstrated in very specific ways that God had a plan and purpose for my life.

I want to thank my family: my wonderful in-laws (Steve and Sue), my dad (Bill) and stepmom (Debbie), my brother and sister-in-law (Mike and Carrie), and my sister (Cora). We have a lot of history together, and I would not be who I am today without you.

Scott and Jenni Wilson are not only our pastors, but, also some of our best friends in the world. Thank you for your consistent love, support, and belief.

I would like to give special thanks to Danny and Maggie Kent. When I was a broken and hurting young man, they loved me well and showed me how to incorporate Christ into every area of my life. Danny was the first person I saw who used his business as a vehicle to reach people for God and his example continues to impact everything I do today.

I would like to thank our wonderful executive team at the John Houston Family of companies: Chad, Terry, Bobby, and Charity as well as the entire JH Family staff for allowing me to lead and love as I listen for God's direction. You know what we say: we're going to make the wisest decision possible unless God tells us to do something different.

This book would not be written without the great work of Dick Parker. I'm grateful for the way he used his gifts to help me tell this story. I want to thank Jonathan Merkh, my publishing partner, for believing in the message of this book. I have so much gratitude for Aunie Brooks and Holly Moore. They have led the efforts to share my God story in a way that hopefully many can understand and be encouraged.

I also want to thank my children, Austin and Ashtyn. Being your dad is one of the greatest blessings in my life. I want you to always remember that you have a faithful and loving Heavenly Father. Each of us have a God story if we follow Him . . . not to perfection . . . but follow Him as He leads us. Remember, He has great hopes, plans, and a future for each of you.

And finally, I thank my wife, Tracy. You are a wonderful woman of God who has loved me through many years of brokenness and hurt, through good times and bad, and during years when I was so hard to love. You are the love of my life, and I thank God every day for the life He has given me with you.